Neo-Confucian Self-Cultivation

Neo-Confucian Self-Cultivation

BARRY C. KEENAN

Dimensions of Asian Spirituality

UNIVERSITY OF HAWAI'I PRESS

Honolulu

DIMENSIONS OF ASIAN SPIRITUALITY
Henry Rosemont, Jr., General Editor

*This series makes available short but comprehensive works on specific Asian
philosophical and religious schools of thought, works focused on a specific region, and
works devoted to the full articulation of a concept central to one or more of Asia's
spiritual traditions. Series volumes are written by distinguished scholars in the field
who not only present their subject matter in historical context for the non-specialist
reader, but also express their own views of the contemporary spiritual relevance
of their subject matter for global citizens of the twenty-first century.*

16 15 14 13 12 11   6 5 4 3 2 1

Library of Congress Cataloging-in-Publication Data
Keenan, Barry C.
Neo-Confucian self-cultivation / Barry C. Keenan.
p.   cm — (Dimensions of Asian spirituality)
Includes bibliographical references and index.
ISBN 978-0-8248-3496-8 (hardcover : alk. paper) —
ISBN 978-0-8248-3548-4 (pbk. : alk. paper)

1. Neo-Confucianism — China — History.   2. Confucian ethics —
China — History.   3. Confucian education — China — History.
I. Title.   II. Series: Dimensions of Asian spirituality.
B127.N4K44   2011
181'.112 — dc22
2011000570

Despite my best efforts, I was unable to locate the owners of the copyrights
to the White Deer Grotto Academy and Yuelu Academy photos. I would be
pleased to include appropriate acknowledgments of which I am
informed in subsequent editions of this book. BK

Printed by Sheridan Books, Inc.

Frontis art: This is the early graph of the verb "to think" in Chinese.
The top of the character is a cranium with something in it. Attached to it is
a heart with ventricles and the aorta visible. The original composition of the
character can be regarded as a symbol of an important characteristic
of Confucian thought: cerebral thinking should
not be detached from the emotions.

A small temple located on the banks of the Stream of Nine Bends in the Wuyi Mountains of northern Fujian Province. Zhu Xi (1130–1200) repeatedly returned to the sanctuary provided by this secluded mountain region to study, teach, and write. (October 2007; courtesy of Deborah Sommer)

Contents

Editor's Preface

ABOUT THIS SERIES

The University of Hawai'i Press has long been noted for its scholarly publications in, and commitment to, the field of Asian Studies. The present volume is the sixth in a series initiated by the press in keeping with that commitment, Dimensions of Asian Spirituality.

It is a most appropriate time for such a series. A number of the world's religions — major and minor — originated in Asia, continue to influence significantly the lives of almost half of the world's peoples, and should now be seen as global in scope, reach, and impact, with rich and varied resources for every citizen of the twenty-first century to explore.

Religion is at the heart of every culture. To be sure, cultures have also been influenced by climate, geology, and the consequent patterns of economic activity they have developed for the production and distribution of goods. Only a very minimal knowledge of physical geography is necessary to understand why African sculptors largely employed wood as their medium while their Italian Renaissance brethren usually worked with marble. But while necessary for understanding cultures — not least our own — matters of geography and economics will not be sufficient. Wood and marble are also found in China, yet Chinese sculptors carved Confucian sages, Daoist immortals, and bodhisattvas from their materials, not *chiwaras* or *pietas*.

In the same way, a mosque, synagogue, cathedral, stupa, and pagoda may be equally beautiful, but they are beautiful in different ways, and the differences cannot be accounted for merely on the basis of the materials used in their construction; their beauty, their ability to inspire awe and to invite contemplation, rests largely on the religious view of the world — and the place of human beings in that world — that inspired and is expressed in their architecture.

Thus the spiritual dimensions of a culture are reflected significantly not only in art and architecture, but in music, myths, poetry, rituals, customs, and patterns of social behavior as well; it follows that if we wish to understand why and how members of other cultures live as they do, we must understand the religious beliefs and practices to which they adhere.

In the first instance, such understanding of the "other" leads to tolerance, which is surely a good thing; much of the pain and suffering in the world today is attributable to intolerance, a fear and hatred of those who look, think, and act differently. But as technological changes in communication, production, and transportation shrink the world, more and more people must confront the fact of human diversity in multiply diverse forms — both between and within nation-states — and hence there is a growing need to go beyond mere tolerance of difference to an appreciation and celebration of it. Tolerance alone cannot contribute substantively to making the world a better — and sustainable — place for human beings to live, the evils attendant on intolerance notwithstanding and not to be minimized. But in an important sense, mere tolerance is easy because it is passive: I can fully respect your right to believe and worship as you wish, associate with whomever, and say what you will simply by ignoring you; you assuredly have a right to speak but not to make me listen.

Yet for most of us who live in economically developed societies or are among the affluent in developing nations, tolerance is not enough; ignoring the poverty, disease, and gross inequalities that afflict fully a third of the human race will only exacerbate, not alleviate, the conditions responsible for the misery that generates the violence becoming ever more commonplace throughout the world today.

Some would have us believe that religion is — as it supposedly always has been — the root cause of the violence and therefore should be done away with. This negative view is reinforced by invoking distorted accounts of the cosmologies of the world's religious heritages and pointing out that they are incompatible with much that we know of the world today from science. These negative accounts, now increasing quantitatively as their quality declines, also suffer from a continued use of the Abrahamic monotheistic religions of the West as a template for all religions, one ill-suited to the particularities of the several Asian spiritual traditions.

Despite the attacks on religion today, it should be clear that they are not going to go away; nor should they. Those who see only the untoward influences — influences not to be ignored — are taking "a printed bill of fare as the equivalent for a solid meal," to quote William James.

Worse than that, to point the finger at religion as responsible for most of the violence worldwide today is to obscure a far more important root cause: poverty. In this view, the violence will cease only when the more fortunate among the peoples of the world become active, not passive; take up the plight of the less fortunate; and resolve to create and maintain a more just world—a resolve that requires a full appreciation of the co-humanity of everyone, significant differences in religious beliefs and practices notwithstanding.

Such appreciation should not, of course, oblige everyone to endorse all of the beliefs and practices followed by adherents of other religions, just as one may object to certain beliefs and practices within one's own faith. A growing number of Catholics, for instance, support a married clergy, the ordination of women, recognition of rights for gays and lesbians, and full reproductive rights for women. Yet they remain Catholics, believing that the tenets of their faith have the conceptual resources to bring about and justify these changes.

In the same way, we can also believe—as a number of Muslim women do—that the Quran and other Islamic theological writings contain the conceptual resources to overcome the inferior status of women in many Muslim countries. And indeed we can believe that every spiritual tradition has within it the resources to counter older practices inimical to the full flourishing of all the faithful—and of the faithful of other traditions as well.

Another reason to go beyond mere tolerance to appreciation and celebration of the many and varied forms of spiritual expression is virtually a truism: the more we look through a window on another culture's beliefs and practices, the more it becomes a mirror of our own (even for those who follow no religious tradition). We must look very carefully and charitably, however, else the reflections become distorted. When studying other religions, most people are strongly inclined to focus on cosmological and ontological questions, asking, What do these people believe about how the world came to be, is, and where it is heading? Do they believe in ghosts? Immortal souls? A creator god?

Answering these and related metaphysical questions is, of course, necessary for understanding and appreciating fully the specific forms and content of the art, music, architecture, rituals, and traditions inspired by the specific religion under study. But the sensitive—and sensible—student will bracket the further question of whether the metaphysical pronouncements are literally true; we must attend carefully to the metaphysics (and theologies) of the religions we study, but questions of their literal truth should be set aside to concentrate on a different question: How could a thoughtful, thoroughly decent human being subscribe to and follow these beliefs and attendant practices?

We may come to see and appreciate how each religious tradition, studied in this light, provides a coherent account of a world not fully amenable to human manipulation, nor perhaps even to full human understanding. The metaphysical pronouncements of the world's religions of course differ measurably from faith to faith, and each has had a significant influence on the physical expressions of the respective faith in synagogues, stupas, mosques, pagodas, and cathedrals. Despite these differences among the buildings, however, the careful and sensitive observer can see the spiritual dimensions of human life that these sacred structures share and express, and in the same way we can come to see and appreciate the common spiritual dimensions of each religion's differing metaphysics and theology. While the several religious traditions give different answers to the question of the meaning of life, they all provide a multiplicity of similar guidelines and spiritual disciplines to enable everyone to find meaning *in* life, in this world.

By plumbing the spiritual depths of other religious traditions, then, we may come to more deeply explore the spiritual resources of our own and at the same time diminish the otherness of the other and create a more peaceable and just world in which all can find meaning in their all-too-human lives.

ABOUT THIS BOOK

The sixth volume in the Dimensions of Asian Spirituality, *Neo-Confucian Self Cultivation,* is a most timely addition to the series in two distinct ways: it describes a scholarly and nontheological spiritual path of direct relevance to Western scholars and students, and thereby also provides a historic, philosophical, and religious background against which the many and varied patterns of intellectual and religious activities comprising the revival of Confucianism in the Peoples' Republic of China (PRC) today might fruitfully be examined and analyzed.

Some scholars in the PRC, for example, want to reexamine both the classical and Neo-Confucian texts against the background of modern

Western philosophy, seeking to integrate the two. Others believe it should be studied only within the context of Chinese culture, because the standard Western philosophical fields — aesthetics, logic, metaphysics, ethics, epistemology, and so on — distort Confucian writings by forcing them into poorly fitting categories (which many believe have decreasing relevance to the global twenty-first century).

Many other Chinese are as much concerned with the *practice* of Confucianism as they are with its more theoretical and scholarly dimensions. Such individuals range from the popularizer Yu Dan — whose book on how Confucianism can help all Chinese today sold eight million copies the year it was published — to the scholar/activist Zhang Xianglong, who wishes to establish "preservation zones" in which Confucianism might be lived by groups who adhere to the tradition without modern scientific and technological distractions, reviving family and clan life, rituals, and classical studies. The inspiration for Zhang's plan was the Amish communities in the United States.

There are also Confucians in China today (and in the diaspora) who would like to make Confucianism one of the state religions recognized by the Bureau of Religious Affairs, and still others who would make it *the* state religion, financially and politically endorsed and supported by the government.

A final current in the contemporary revival of Confucianism is the reestablishment of Confucian academies — special centers of learning that have no close counterparts in Western education — which gives this book great immediacy as well as more general currency for understanding Chinese intellectual life today. Barry Keenan engages both classical Confucian texts and the writings of their Neo-Confucian successors, especially as found in the works of Zhu Xi and, to a lesser extent, Wang Yangming. At the heart of his exposition is the *Daxue* (Great Learning), the shortest of all Confucian writings but also one of the most influential. Keenan describes and analyzes with sensitivity and acumen the way the text served as the basis for all self-cultivation practices engaged in by the Confucians for almost a millennium beginning in the eleventh century CE and lasting until the end of the last dynasty in 1911 — and now being instituted anew a century later.

Moreover, Keenan has himself taught the texts and the Neo-Confucian practices based on them to his students for more than a decade, in the same way students were taught in the Neo-Confucian academies for centuries, which makes his book come alive in a most engaging pedagogic fashion for all interested in religious theory and practices, not just Confucianism. He recounts as well the lives and (often very horrible) deaths of several exemplars of the tradition, inspiration no less for everyone today than for the Chinese literati of centuries past, as Keenan makes clear throughout his narrative.

In sum, *Neo-Confucian Self Cultivation* deals in an integrated way with Chinese history, philosophy, religion, and pedagogy throughout much of the sweep of the cultural heritage, especially from the Song through the Qing periods. Keenan makes abundantly clear that the Confucians were much more than civil servants, much more concerned with substance than with form, and have much to teach us all today.

Dynastic Periods in Chinese History

BEFORE THE COMMON ERA (BCE)

Shang (Yin) dynasty	1570–1045
Zhou dynasty	1045–221
Spring and Autumn Period	771–479
Warring States Period	479–221
(100 Schools of Thought)	
Qin dynasty	221–206

THE COMMON ERA (CE)

Han dynasty	202 BCE–220 CE
Western Han	202 BCE–9 CE
Eastern Han	25 CE–220 CE
Six Dynasties	220–589
Sui dynasty	589–617
Tang dynasty	617–907
Five Dynasties	907–960
Song dynasty	960–1279
Northern Song	960–1126
Southern Song	1126–1279
Yuan (Mongol) dynasty	1279–1368
Ming dynasty	1368–1644
Qing (Manchu) dynasty	1644–1911

Preface

My interest in the moral and spiritual doctrine of self-cultivation arose from watching the classical Confucian texts come alive in the hands of college students. I wondered in those courses why the Neo-Confucian academy pedagogy I had adopted, such as personal journals, seemed to fit so appropriately with the way the classical texts themselves were composed. Tutorials on student journal entries that commented on passages from the classics transformed my role somewhat mysteriously from Confucian academy headmaster into simply a fellow student of the texts. One reason was the largely unedited and anecdotal organization of passages in some early Confucian texts that invited the experience of each reader to determine the relevance of passages in his or her own life.

The Dimensions of Asian Spirituality book series is designed to provide a reader-friendly narrative appropriate for both college students and the general reader. For that reason, only direct quotations are referenced. I have also included at the end of this volume a list of Further Readings that indicates valuable secondary sources for those who wish to pursue issues further. Translations designated in the Further Readings section to be used throughout the text are always cited unless an exception is indicated in the body of the text. A "Chronology of Works and Thinkers with the Correct Sequence for Reading the Four Books Indicated" appears as an appendix.

Three alternative literatures and discourses are cited in this book. First, historical discourse contextualizes the Neo-Confucian movement and the development over time of its sophisticated form of self-cultivation. Second, Sinology, that laudable interdisciplinary study of China that can provide analysis of an excavated text with philological care, is called upon when needed. Finally, philosophical discourse is called upon to define Neo-Confucian epistemology and metaphysics, although they are not the main theme of this study. In some of the chapters that follow all three discourses will appear.

As is the Chinese tradition, surnames precede given names in this text; hence in the name Wang Yangming, for example, Wang is the surname and Yangming the given name.

Acknowledgments

More than ten years of seminar students at Denison University convinced me this book should be written. I thank the students in each seminar for their rich interaction with the texts and with one another.

Nonfiction, much like modern Confucian self-cultivation, is not a lone enterprise. Henry Rosemont, Jr., has edited with the clarity of Socrates and the passion of Wang Yangming. His conviction regarding the equality of Asian thought in academia is so strong it generates disciples. My warm appreciation to him.

Two friends have been quite close to the composition of this manuscript: Scott Duncanson, a gifted wordsmith with unusual abilities in Asian materials, and Richard Lucier, a wise man. To both friends, please accept my lasting gratitude.

I would also like to extend my sincere appreciation to several others whose support has been invaluable: first, for their advice, Ted de Bary (especially for suggesting "recognize" as an upgraded translation of the term *gé wu*), Joseph Adler, Lao Yan-shuan, and Tu Weiming; second, for consultation, Daniel K. Gardner, Andrew Hsieh, Lian Xinda, C. T. Hu, Peter K. Bol, Roger T. Ames, Peng Guoxiang, and Stephen Angle; and third, for clarifications, Karen Towslee (later Keenan), Tony and Pat Stoneburner, Jack Stanitz, David Anderson, Mark Chen-Keenan, Mark Belletini, James M. Dunn, Richard Dawson, Karen Watts, Maylon Hepp, and David De Villiers. A great copy editor is a gift, and I thank Susan Biggs Corrado for her many skills.

I would like to thank the Robert C. Good and Lilly Endowment funds administered by Denison University for their financial support of research leaves. To the Education Program of the East-West Center in Honolulu, my appreciation for office space and the opportunity to present chapters.

For her remarkable patience and moral support, special gratitude to my wife, Karen Lynne Keenan.

Introduction

This book tells the story of the moral and spiritual practice of Neo-Confucian self-cultivation in Chinese history. The heart of the program of self-cultivation will be revealed by opening up its essential texts and analyzing how they should be studied. Travel with me back to the year 1000 CE when our story begins with the arrival of the new intellectual and political movement called Neo-Confucianism. We end our journey in 1911 — a time when Neo-Confucian self-cultivation was embedded for the last time in the inherited Confucian social and political institutions of imperial China.

Neo-Confucianism, at its origins in the Song period, held that moral authority could exist independently of current power holders. The earliest Neo-Confucians believed that this insight had been lost following the death of the philosopher Mencius (ca. 380–290 BCE) and remained lost until the rehabilitation of the Learning of the Way (Daoxue) in the early eleventh century. A ruler might want to claim inherited virtue or knowledge as a source of political authority, but Neo-Confucians were convinced that rulers, like scholar-officials and literati, had to self-cultivate in order to generate virtue, knowledge, and, hence, moral authority.

After 1000 CE Neo-Confucians perfected a means of self-cultivation based on the schematic outline contained in a brief, neglected classical text called the *Great Learning* that laid out the steps of self-transformation. The first four steps of personal cultivation described in the text can be thought of as sequential practices: (1) Recognize [investigate] Things and Affairs; (2) Extend One's Knowing; and (3) Make One's Intentions Sincere to (4) Rectify One's Mind. Neo-Confucians assumed that the steps were written by Confucius and that most of the attached commentary explaining each step was composed by the senior disciple of Confucius, Zengzi (505–436). Zengzi's commentary for step 3, for example, reads,

> One allows no self-deception, just as when one hates a hateful smell
> or loves a lovely color. This is called being content within oneself,

and this is why the exemplary person must be watchful over himself in solitude. The petty person, when living alone, is quite without restraint in doing what is not good. As soon as he sees an exemplary person he moves to dissemble, concealing what is not good and making a display of what is good. The other sees right away through him, as if seeing his lungs and liver. Of what use is his dissembling? This is a case of what is truly within being manifested without, and this is why the exemplary person must be watchful over himself in solitude.[1]

Like a gemologist who cuts, chisels, polishes, and buffs a rough gem, these initial steps of personal development describe a process necessary to bring perfection to the precious stone of human conduct.

The self-cultivating person emerges from this practice of the first four steps and can move forward to step 5, Cultivate the Person, at which point one can be said to have established his or her own moral values and moral voice. Reciprocal interpersonal trust is built in this step because personal cultivation is carried out through relationships with others. The morally cultivated person leads by example, and the final three steps of the eight-step program of self-cultivation are tangible ways in which society can organize itself around interactions of this mutual trust: (6) Regulate the Family, (7) Order the State, and (8) Bring Peace to All.

No single manual exists in Chinese that analyzes the varying ways an individual should self-cultivate. Instead, teachers would have gradually inculcated these methods throughout the Neo-Confucian curriculum that a student had followed from childhood. But the advice Song Neo-Confucians gave the emperor was very clearly to study the Eight Steps in the *Great Learning*. Part II of this book puts into English the careful way Song Neo-Confucian philosophers felt this should be done. Because later students of the Neo-Confucian canon of texts would need some guidance in following these steps in their own lives, an anthology of the founding masters of Neo-Confucianism was published in 1175 and is cited extensively in Part II to flesh out the practice of each step.

A technique commonly used by Neo-Confucians working on the practice of self-cultivation was to keep a daily diary of their thoughts and interactions. As the renowned Japanese Confucian Kaibara Ekken

(1630–1714) described his practice, "At night we reflect on our mistakes during the day, and if there are no failings we can sleep peacefully. If there are failings we should be repentant and ashamed and take this as the lesson for the following day."[2] Indeed, in China there are nineteenth-century records of powerful governors of provinces and other high officials who managed thousands of people and who chose to meet regularly in small coteries of around three or four friends to maintain their self-cultivation by exchanging their private diaries. Once exchanged, the close friends would make marginal comments about the decisions, worries, or temptations noted in another friend's diary. This form of self-cultivation involved both solitary contemplation and respectful interaction.

Neo-Confucian self-cultivation bases moral action on hard work in human relations. Reverence (*jing*) in human relations is one capacity that motivates and generates in us the appropriate practical responses to the many moral situations we face. This deeply respectful attitude toward one's social interactions accompanied the entire eight-step program and can be considered an independent technique of self-cultivation. Reverence can emerge from the sense of awe one experiences from feeling one is on the path of humaneness (*ren*) — even if we see that moral path for only a short time. Finally, attaining the state of being called humaneness (*ren*) requires a lifetime of self-cultivation and results in moral action that has by then become second nature. Our earliest glimpses of living on a moral plane can corroborate the possibility and the power of mutual reverence for one another. Practiced regularly, the work of reverence entails the ability to materialize in our behavior such feelings as deference, respect, shame, awe, doing one's utmost on behalf of others, honesty, kindness, and courage, as each of these becomes appropriate to the moral requirements of the situations we face.

One article of faith in the ideology of the first Neo-Confucians was that human nature is innately good. Curiously, the modern scientific field of evolutionary biology provides interesting support for this persistent position in Neo-Confucian ethics. Biologists have found that natural selection over generations of evolution has genetically conditioned *Homo sapiens* to be born with mutually beneficial instincts that we naturally practice among our relatives. These include empathy, self-respect, humility, and selfless humaneness. The philosopher

Donald Munro has recently shown the significant compatibility of these findings with the capacity for goodness in the Mencian strain of classical Confucianism that informed the Neo-Confucian intellectual movement.

Throughout later Chinese history, scholar-officials and, more broadly, the attentive and prestigious moral elite (*shidafu*) consistently referred back to the sophisticated formulation of Song dynasty self-cultivation that itself built upon classical Confucianism. Starting from an empathy that builds one's moral self by reaching out to others, and expanding by observing personal reverence and civility in relationships, Neo-Confucian ethics begins and ends in a this-worldly commitment to humaneness that is sustained through human interaction. Achieving humaneness remained the objective of Confucian ethics until the last dynasty fell in 1911.

The single most important figure in the consolidation of Neo-Confucianism as a doctrine was Zhu Xi (pronounced "djew shee"; 1130–1200), who lived under political conditions that forced him again and again to seek refuge in academic life. This made him the first in a continuing series of Neo-Confucian moral exemplars who fought against overwhelming odds to bring morality into power. He was recommended for public service more than once and did venture into official positions, only to find his criticisms of corrupt practices unacceptable to established power holders. Personal integrity and intellectual brilliance were constant throughout his life, and in the end it was through his writings that his moral vision was fully vindicated. His scholarship found a channel of expression that had political significance and influence for a consistent six hundred–year period.

Zhu Xi's personal story became public at the precocious age of eighteen, when he achieved the equivalent of a doctoral degree, thus qualifying him for scholar-official status. He then served as magistrate in Tongan County in the southern province of Fujian with extraordinary results; his leadership skills garnered tremendous praise from the residents. In 1162 the newly enthroned Xiaozong emperor (r. 1162–1189) sent out a call for advice regarding how to handle the invading Jurchen aggressors from across China's northern border, and Zhu, now thirty-one, sent a sealed memorial in response. He soon received an imperial summons to the capital and had three meetings with the emperor, during which he counseled him to work on the initial steps of the *Great*

Learning as a personal practice, to listen to the people, and above all to not capitulate to the territorial claims of the Jurchen. Zhu's suggested strategy was to wage a cold war against the Jurchen so that the emperor would have time to strengthen the country internally. But venal advisors refused his advice, and Zhu himself was offered an appointment to teach in the national military academy, which he rejected. Returning to the province of his youth, Fujian, he turned to academic work for the next fourteen years.

As a scholar Zhu very keenly analyzed the most subtle of the Neo-Confucian philosophers of the preceding century and began writing moral philosophy as it was normally done in imperial China — as commentaries on existing classics. It is clear from his writing that by age thirty-eight Zhu's academic work was dedicated to promoting the Neo-Confucian views of his predecessors, the brothers Cheng Hao (1032–1085) and Cheng Yi (1033–1077) and their uncle, Zhang Zai (1020–1077). By age forty-five Zhu had composed with a friend, Lü Zuqian, an anthology, *Reflections on Things at Hand,* that included their choices of the great Neo-Confucian thinkers from the eleventh century. *Reflections* provided the thematic outline for Neo-Confucian compilations to be used by examination candidates in later centuries, such as *The Great Collection of Neo-Confucianism* (*Xingli dachuan*) of 1415 and the 1715 official anthology of Neo-Confucian thinkers in the Qing dynasty (1644–1911), *Essential Ideas of [the Cheng-Zhu school of] Nature and Principle* (*Xingli jingyi*). In his lifetime Zhu Xi produced almost one hundred serious works of scholarship comprising twenty-seven thick modern volumes when published in the terse Chinese script.

At the age of forty-nine, after twice having refused an appointment to manage a three-county prefecture, Zhu finally accepted. However, instead of using available funds on the official public schools with their vocational objectives, he rebuilt a Neo-Confucian academy that had been replaced earlier by public schools. Zhu insisted that the Song court finance this project and others that were independent of the vocational aims of the state. The result, White Deer Grotto Academy, became a model for outstanding Confucian academies down to the nineteenth century. Relentless in moral courage, Zhu, at age fifty, sent a sealed memorial to the Xiaozong emperor pointing out a second time the connection between the moral development of a ruler and the economic, military, and political health of his country. And by

(*Above and facing page*) White Deer Grotto Academy. Originally founded in 940 CE, Zhu Xi reconstructed the academy in 1179 CE. Location and date: Lushan, Jiangxi Province, as the site was preserved at the end of the twentieth century. The four photos are of the main entrance gate, with "White

Deer Grotto Academy" inscribed in characters, a building in the academy complex (lower left), an internal gateway (upper right), and stone statuary of a white deer in front of an inscribed stone stele. (From *Zhongguo Shuyuan Cidian,* ed. Ji Xiaofeng [Hangzhou: Zhejiang Jiaoyu Chubanshe, 1996])

age fifty-eight Zhu had cashiered several corrupt officials under his jurisdiction and confronted the emperor during two more personal audiences, repeating his message regarding the court's role in allowing wicked officials to be appointed.

Refusing another uninteresting appointment offered by the court, Zhu withdrew once again to the solitude of the Wuyi Mountains in northern Fujian Province. There he built the Wuyi Retreat nestled below the awesome rock formations of the Stream of Nine Bends, a place for him to reside and write, as well as discuss scholarship with students and visitors. (The cover of this book has a picture of a small temple on this stream today.) Zhu called his retreat, which could be reached only by boat, "a heaven outside of the human world."

At age sixty-four, two events in Zhu's life had lasting effects. First, he took a three-month post in western China, where he set a pattern in educational institutions for the spread of Neo-Confucianism through several provinces. During the three months that Zhu held authority in Changsha City, he lectured at Yuelu Academy, a decaying edifice of some note where much earlier he and Zhang Shi (1133–1180) had lectured and whose reputation he had helped advance. He posted the "Articles for Learning" there from White Deer Grotto Academy, and with great persistence he obtained the financing that made renovation of the academy possible. His presence and his efforts immediately attracted many good scholars from the region, thus breathing new life into the academy. Zhu's educational objective was not scholarly mastery, but the development of moral autonomy. Learning was personal moral growth in the best Neo-Confucian academies. Therefore, when the graduates of the White Deer Grotto and Yuelu Academies founded new academies that spread Neo-Confucian ideas throughout China for years to come, so went the message: moral authority emanates from self-cultivation.

When a new emperor ascended the throne in 1194, Zhu Xi received an appointment as Junior Lecturer-in-Waiting upon the recommendation of his friend, the prime minister. Zhu accepted and again lectured on the *Great Learning* at court, but he also attacked an imperial relative as corrupt. The consequences were severe. Zhu was dismissed from his new post, and the prime minister was even accused of conspiracy.

In the last five years of Zhu's life factions around the emperor finally turned their anger at Zhu into an attack on his "false learning" and pointedly proscribed the writings of the Neo-Confucian mentors he had endorsed. Nine other crimes were listed in an impeachment document by a court censor, and Zhu then lost even the governmental sinecures that allowed him to support his scholarship. One of his disciples was also exiled. Zhu returned one final time to his retreat in the mountains as attacks on his "false learning" intensified. He died in poverty in 1200 CE.

Zhu Xi's life was a heroic struggle to connect virtue to power, and although he suffered many defeats in his lifetime, his extraordinary scholarship resulted in a posthumous victory. His scholarship was so impressive that even before the Song period was over, his name was rehabilitated and admitted into the revered Confucian Temple. While his moral leadership was not given official authority during his lifetime, his writings later reemerged to become the national standard for official recruitment. In 1212 the Song court allowed state schools to make available his remarkable commentaries on the *Analects* and the *Mencius*. In 1313 the Yuan dynasty, run by the Mongols, bestowed upon him the most ironic but meaningful honor for a man who had resisted foreign rule all his life: Zhu's commentaries interpreting the meaning of the classics were approved and soon became required reading for all candidates for the civil service examinations. The following Ming dynasty did the same in 1415, and in 1715, when China's final dynasty, the Qing, published its anthology of Neo-Confucian thinkers, it reaffirmed Zhu's commentaries as the official basis for its civil service examinations. Thus for nearly six hundred continuous years after 1313, Zhu Xi's Neo-Confucian interpretation of the classics had biblical authority for all civil service examination candidates aspiring to scholar-official status.

Once it was formulated as an ethical program that any scholar-official could follow, Neo-Confucianism generated critics who were free to openly attack any deception by government, misuse of its power, or the inveterate corruption of the centralized bureaucratic state. The story of the second most famous Neo-Confucian thinker, Wang Yangming (1472–1529), reveals both his moral courage and the fearsome power of retribution by officials under attack. A young Wang had been qualified for scholar-official status only seven years when he witnessed a shocking event in court politics: two officials had been unjustly imprisoned by a eunuch, the hidden power behind the throne.

(*Above and facing page*) Yuelu Academy. Founded in 976 CE, Zhu Xi held scholarly discussions at Yuelu Academy in 1167 CE and briefly taught there in 1194 CE. Location and date: Changsha City on the modern campus of Hunan University, Hunan Province, as the site was preserved at the end of the twentieth century. The four photos include the main entrance (upper left), two buildings in the academy complex, and the reconstructed headmaster's residence (lower right). (From *Zhongguo Shuyuan Cidian,* ed. Ji Xiaofeng [Hangzhou: Zhejiang Jiaoyu Chubanshe, 1996])

Trying to correct the injustice, Wang spoke out firmly to defend them. For his temerity Wang was publically flogged into unconsciousness, then exiled to a frontier region, Dragon Field in Guizhou Province.

En route to this remote region, Wang had to evade assassins sent by the eunuch by pretending to drown himself. He managed to survive the trip to Dragon Field, but because death by disease or wild animal was an ever-present threat, and because he lived in constant fear of assassination, he decided, at the age of thirty-six, to build a stone coffin for himself. At a low point, Wang meditated frequently, and in the process happened to gain a radically new philosophic insight into Neo-Confucian doctrine. Eventually, his revelation regarding the critical role of the heart-and-mind (*xin*) in how we become moral human beings would initiate an entire subfield of Neo-Confucianism. After years of exile Wang returned to public life when the political climate changed and became a charismatic lecturer, a theoretician propounding his insightful understanding of Neo-Confucian thought, and even a renowned general.

Heroic personal histories of moral courage punctuate the story of Neo-Confucianism in Chinese history. Zhu Xi and Wang Yangming stood up when power lost its connection to virtue, and suffered the consequences. Unfortunately, leaders today face parallel problems that continue to plague the present: once someone is in a position of significant power, there is always the temptation to bend or break the rules by which one gained such power. The strength of Neo-Confucian self-cultivation was to provide a program of personal learning and moral transformation that made available to individuals the final remaining resource: self-restraint.

PART I

Neo-Confucianism, 1000—1400

CHAPTER 1

Song Dynasty Neo-Confucianism

The intellectual movement known as Neo-Confucianism, begun in the eleventh century, developed one of the most sophisticated formulations of self-cultivation in the history of humanistic education. After looking at its historical background, I will treat the three components that made its doctrines new: (1) the reshaping of what constituted the Confucian canon of texts; (2) the metaphysical assumption that there are underlying principles existing independently of the knower, in all things, affairs, and our innately good human nature; and (3) an elaborated program of self-cultivation. The remarkable Song dynasty synthesis of these three components defining how to live humanely changed organically within the institutions of imperial China until the fall of China's last dynasty in 1911.

Historical Background:
Classical and Imperial Confucianism

Confucius (551–479 BCE) witnessed the death throes of aristocracy in ancient China. His teachings called for an aristocracy of moral merit or talent to replace the anarchic feuding of small states that was beginning the Warring States Period (479–221). But instead the Qin (pronounced "chin") state, which gave China its name in the West, gobbled up its competitors "as a silkworm consuming mulberry leaves." The political philosophy of legalism that enabled the first emperor of Qin to force unification in 221 BCE explicitly rejected the system of aristocratic inheritance, but it was unlike Confucian doctrine in its reliance upon ruthless authority.

While politically chaotic, the Warring States Period was so culturally productive that it became informally called the Period of the One Hundred Schools of Thought. The political and social disruptions of the many contending states brought forward a number of thinkers, most of whom were wrestling with the confusion of a disintegrating social order. Confucius himself never held office long enough during those unstable times to convince a potentate officially to implement his ideas in even one small state, but his seventy-two immediate disciples began a lineage of ideas that has not gone away. When Confucius died it appears he felt his life and work had been ineffective, and he seemingly had no sense that his analysis of human nature would be of such lasting value to individuals and rulers thereafter. Then, about one hundred years following China's forced unification in 221 BCE, Confucian ethics were stretched to become an imperial political ideology under the Han dynasty (202 BCE–220 CE), and dynastic governments thereafter found it useful to reassert this form of imperialized Confucianism down to the twentieth century.

Confucius taught any serious student, no matter his social background, during his long life, but the master-disciple relationships he established did not leave written texts from the hand of the Master. It is assumed that Confucius' most senior disciple, Zengzi (or possibly another protégé), began soliciting Confucius' sayings from other followers after his death, thereby preserving his teachings. This process did not end with the original disciples, and a composite text was expanded for some 150 years by the Confucian school in the Master's home state of Lu. Some of the exchanges recorded in the collection, called the *Analects* in English (taken from the Greek *analekta,* or selections), are between accomplished disciples. Zengzi was later credited with also writing a philosophic commentary on the short classic the *Great Learning,* which, over a millennium later, became the single most important work in Neo-Confucian education.

Zengzi also apparently took on the responsibility of educating Zisi (d. 402 BCE), Confucius' grandson, since Confucius' son had preceded him in death. The grandson was traditionally said to have led the continuing Confucian School in the third generation after the death of Zengzi. Newly excavated texts attributed to the grandson and his followers suggest a continuing connection directly to the great Confucian thinker Mengzi, who lived 150 years after Confucius. This systematic thinker, known as Mencius in the West, wrote a clear volume called *Mencius* that developed Confucian ethics and also became a significant source of inspiration for Neo-Confucians.

Imperial Confucianism as an official ideology in the Han dynasty was formulated to both justify and make more functional the concentrated power of the empire's small elite. But to do so it added supernatural ideas to the largely personal ethics of Confucius that he himself would not have recognized. These changes were hoped to be useful in protecting bureaucrats from the despotic power of the royal family and the inner court attached to it, but the assumption that Heaven might send signs to indicate the justice or injustice of the emperor's policies was a political manipulation of original Confucian ideas. Despite such distortions, a lasting tradition began during the Han empire whereby a set of Confucian texts was used to prepare recruits to become officials. This formal training and selection of scholar-officials was reinforced again when the Sui-Tang (589–907 CE) dynastic unification reestablished the imperial state after a period of disunity. The first national civil service examination system based on a canon of Confucian texts was instituted in 606 CE. For the next thirteen hundred years the increasingly dominant means of social mobility in one dynasty after another was scholar-official status gained through the civil service examination system. This marriage of academic study and government service lasted until the abolition of the examination system in 1905.

Literati Enter Stage Right

What made the principled actors of the Neo-Confucian movement think they should have a role on China's national political stage? Zhu Xi's massive industry and intellect were indispensable in defining the movement, but let us note that he synthesized the philosophic accomplishments of five great Neo-Confucians who wrote during the one hundred years before Zhu's birth in 1130 CE. These five men were of the literati (*shi*) class and will be discussed further below. With no hereditary aristocracy making the transition from the Tang to Song society, many virtuous, learned men of the literati class took early opportunities to be heard solely on the merits of their ideas. But central government power soon intervened, and in the eleventh century the Five Masters found their writings proscribed by officials close to the emperor who attempted to institute a set of centralized reforms. These New Policies reforms, however, collapsed after only fifty years when a foreign people from the north, the Jurchens, overthrew the Song

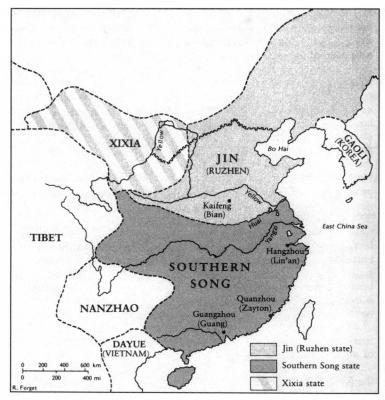

The Southern Song and Jin (Ruzhen) empires in 1142. (Reprinted by permission of the publisher from *China: A New History,* by John King Fairbank, [Cambridge, Mass.: The Belknap Press of Harvard University Press], 116, Copyright © 1992 by the President and Fellows of Harvard College)

dynasty in 1126, forcing the government's disastrous retreat from the Chinese capital of Kaifeng behind the protective moats of the Huai and Yangzi Rivers to Hangzhou (Lin'an) in the south (see map).

The court of the reestablished Southern Song felt forced to accept the Jurchen conquerors' claim to northern China, but this policy decision made many Neo-Confucian literati dig in their heels in resistance to the court's capitulation to the invaders. The Neo-Confucians were politically conservative in resisting the authority of the Southern Song because they based their opposition on a larger conception of the emperorship that had been in existence since the founding of the Song: Neo-Confucians saw Confucius' compilation of *The Spring and Autumn Annals* in his lifetime as proof that he believed informed moral learning should challenge and replace rule based on power alone. The *Annals* were read as demonstrating that Confucius believed the earliest states at the origins of Chinese civilization (preceding Confucius) had collapsed because sages were not in power. This line of argument, applied to the present, justified the leadership of virtuous literati as alternative voices to the absolute authority claimed by an emperor who, they added, had been justified solely on a presumed mandate from Heaven that was, in fact, simply hereditary rule.

This political position implied that all emperors were obligated to self-cultivate and attempt to reach sagehood for the good of everyone. Since most emperors in the past had not developed moral authority through self-cultivation and had illicitly claimed to possess a continuing mandate from the founder of their dynasties, they actually were more or less managers who received the support of the people according to their competence. Notice also that Neo-Confucian literati might well qualify for elite political status without office under this argument because of their personal moral development. The political position of the Neo-Confucians during the Southern Song was that scholar-official government should replace the imperial ideal and that effective social transformation should legitimately take place in strong local communities under literati leadership.

What Was New in Neo-Confucianism?

The Five Masters of the Northern Song (before the government was forced southward by invaders) — Zhou Dunyi (1010–1073), the brothers Cheng Hao and Cheng Yi, their uncle Zhang Zai, and their close friend Shao Yong (1011–1077) — were scholars committed to personal learning over their own eminence in public office. Their teachings, which were consolidated by the great Southern Song sage and scholar Zhu Xi two generations later, were the basis of the three traits that typified the origins of Neo-Confucianism: (1) the reshaping of what constituted the canon of Confucian classics; (2) the philosophical doctrine that added metaphysical ideas to classical Confucian thought; and (3) an elaborated program of self-cultivation.

While Zhu's work in merging the Five Masters' positions, along with his own teachings, influenced many literati of his generation to shift to the Neo-Confucian position, one acquaintance, Lu Xiangshan (1139–1193), differed with Zhu on important details of doctrine, and that difference perpetuated itself as a separate current within the Neo-Confucian mainstream (discussed below).

The Reshaped Canon of Classics

In defining which texts would constitute the orthodox Confucian canon, Neo-Confucian scholars added the Four Books as equal in importance to the Five Classics, which had been the voice of Confucian ethics for the preceding thousand years. The *Classic of Changes* (*Yijing*), the *Classic of Documents* (*Shujing*), the *Classic of Odes* (*Shijing*), the *Spring and Autumn Annals* (*Chunqiu*), and the *Record of Rites* (*Liji*) were considered authoritative statements of philosophy, history, poetry, and ritual. The four "new" classics — the *Great Learning*, the *Analects*, the *Mencius*, and the *Mean* — represented a shift away from values derived from ritualized social practice and toward an emphasis on the innate sources of human morality. The Four Books allowed, and even encouraged, a natural focus on the moral and spiritual development of a person. As systematized by Zhu Xi, the books were meant to be read sequentially, and he appended commentaries explaining the meaning of every important passage: a student should first read the *Great Learning*, then the *Analects*, then the *Mencius*, and finally the *Mean*.

The first of the Four Books, the *Great Learning*, had originally been tucked away as chapter 42 of the *Record of Rites* during the classical era. Only about one page long, this insightful text succinctly connected personal cultivation to good governance. By reading it first, students were able to learn the outline of how self-cultivation could lead to peace in the world. The original text as found in the *Record of Rites* had explanatory commentary on only six of the eight steps that connected personal cultivation to world peace, but Zhu boldly took guidance from the writings of Cheng Yi to add a chapter to the original commentary of Confucius' disciple, Zengzi. Some Neo-Confucians at the time did not accept this elaboration on the text and commentary of an ancient classic because it altered the meaning of the text. But the *Great Learning* with Zhu's additional commentary nevertheless remained the touchstone for self-cultivation to most later Neo-Confucians.

In the *Analects,* the next book in the sequence, students found moral examples in dialogue form that were easily accessible by simply assuming the role of one participant in a conversation. Confucius adapted his advice to the learning styles of different disciples in a very personal way. For example, once, in giving contradictory answers to the same questions, Confucius explained, "Ranyou is diffident, and so I urged him on. But Zilu has the energy of two, so I sought to rein him in" (*Analects* 11.22). Students therefore could easily relate to these first-person stories of live interactions. Cheng Hao had taught in the Northern Song that Mencius' brilliant statements could not serve the needs of novice ethics students as well as the personal stories in the *Analects* did — those stories demonstrated how Confucius' disciples actually worked on self-cultivation each day.

Perhaps more importantly, the incisive comments of the Master to his students in the *Analects* made the book particularly appropriate for a personalized understanding by a new reader. As comments in the text were addressed to the moral development of disciples, student readers in any era could take the place of the original disciples, and the passages then applied to the new students. It was also true that the perceptive comments about human nature made by Confucius and his followers took on different meanings depending on the life experience a reader brought to the text. The humility clearly evident in Confucius himself provided a constant model for Neo-Confucian readers of how correctly to reveal one's innate moral potential.

Within the pages of the *Mencius,* on the other hand, a student found political advice. Here Mencius actually interviewed kings in at least three of the Warring States about 150 years after the death of Confucius and sternly advised that humaneness and rightness, as built-in capacities of the human condition, are superior to profit or power and thus would develop into a more lasting strength for a political leader. Mencius argued that a selfish, power-hungry monarch would in turn model raw ambition and covetousness for lower officials, thus fostering disloyalty. Similarly, the monarch's neglect of the needs of the people could lead to righteous rebellion. The autocratic first emperor of the Ming dynasty (r. 1368–1399) could not tolerate the criticism implicit in this classic, so he censored eighty-five passages in the *Mencius* to remove them from view of his scholar-officials. Such an action worked for his reign, but the passages were restored some fifteen years after his death.

The *Mean*, the final book in the sequence, was more advanced than the other three books of the basic Neo-Confucian canon. Ideally, by the time students had applied the *Mean* to their lives, deceit or falsity should have been removed from their behavior. The *Mean's* perceptive use of metaphors makes it the most philosophically inspiring of the Four Books. The morally exemplary person is portrayed in the *Mean* as having realized his inner nature and having achieved a level of spiritual development in which that person is able to commune with nature. The *Mean* alone develops overarching issues such as the cosmic connections of Heaven and Earth to sage-like conduct.

Beyond the Four Books, there were two earlier classics considered important in Neo-Confucian training, the first being one of the above-mentioned Five Classics, the *Classic of Changes*. Its text marshaled the wisdom of former sages to help readers understand one's proper response to a specific situation. The second book, the *Rites of Zhou* (*Zhouli*), was assumed in the Song era to be the actual composition of the Duke of Zhou, who was the brother of King Wu (the Zhou took over China in 1045 BCE) and who had selflessly mentored his nephew for seven years as heir-apparent when King Wu died. Various anthologies were also important in the process of Neo-Confucian education.

Neo-Confucian Thought

The addition of metaphysical ideas is the second trait defining Neo-Confucianism. Here a discussion of philosophy is necessary to clarify Neo-Confucian innovations. The reshaping of the classical Confucian canon was initiated by a group of eleventh-century scholars who advocated the Learning of the Way (Daoxue). According to Cheng Yi, it was his older brother, Cheng Hao, who first realized that the ancient classics revealed metaphysically real principles in the world, and it was their uncle, Zhang Zai, who analyzed the dynamics of material force and pointed out that the "principle" (*li*) embedded in matter could be revealed with careful investigation carried out by human learning.

The Neo-Confucian assumption regarding the existence of principle was simple: there is a reason why all things are as they are. Because every object, relationship, and political interaction can also have a reason for why it is as it is, the notion of principle exists everywhere in the universe. The pattern, or web, of principles underlying things and events constitutes a coherent and orderly whole, and that order in the cosmos is shared because all things have principles; while principle is one, its manifestations are many.

Mainstream advocates of the Learning of the Way provided a metaphysical underpinning to classical Confucian ethics, but the moral principles presumed to be innate in our natures were always embedded in *qi,* or material force. *Qi* can be conceived as matter that includes the energy contained within that matter. I do not mean to say that these thinkers were precursors of Albert Einstein's equation of energy and matter, but only that they saw in matter what can be called a dynamic or material force. The quality of the material force endowed in us at birth is different in each person, but it could be refined to make our innate moral principles more accessible. Moral learning and regular self-cultivation can increasingly put us in touch with the original nature in us all — the pure principle that we all share in our natures at birth.

Many of the formulators of Neo-Confucianism took seriously in their own lives the indigenous Chinese philosophic and religious school of Daoism, as well as the imported religion of Buddhism, which came from India to China about 100 CE. Modern scholars of philosophy have demonstrated that the earlier Daoist vocabulary used to translate Buddhist terms from Sanskrit into Chinese resulted in significant changes to Buddhism called Sinified Buddhism. In particular, the Indian Buddhist understanding of the ignorance that the "self" imposes on the illusory reality of things in the world did not survive being filtered through the Daoist vocabulary in China. One result was that the popular Chan (Japanese Zen) school of Chinese Buddhism in the Song dynasty assumed a very un-Indian conception of eliminating selfish and false understandings so that one might *reveal one's innate and perfect Buddha-nature* that lay within human nature.

The effect of this indirect Daoist influence on Confucianism was possible because of the popularity of Chinese Buddhism among Chinese intellectuals. Human nature in Neo-Confucianism was formulated as having two fundamental aspects: a pure and original mode of the mind that Chinese Buddhists called one's Buddha-nature, and an adulterated mode of mind that Neo-Confucians called one's material nature, as opposed to one's original nature. Neo-Confucians reread the ancient Confucian texts in order to detect these newly added distinctions, so the task of self-cultivation became to refine one's material nature to recover the more pure form underneath.

Zhu Xi cited the "Counsels of the Great Yu" passage from the *Classic of Documents,* respected by his Northern Song mentors, to drive home the distinction between the mind of the Way (*dao xin*) and the human mind (*ren xin*). Zhu cited this sixteen-word formula in his "Preface to the *Mean,*" even though he suspected that someone had forged the passage found in the Old Text version of the *Classic of Documents* that had supposedly been rediscovered in the fourth century. The passage clarified the new epistemology of principle.

> The human mind is precarious,
> The mind of the Way is barely perceptible.
> Be discriminating, be one [with the mind of the Way,]
> Hold fast the Mean![1]

While not specific in how to gain the more pure learning, the opening lines of the formula make clear that common apprehension through the human mind would not always expose the full nature of reality.

However, there was a prominent dissenter from Zhu Xi's philosophical position at that time. Lu Xiangshan, an awe-inspiring Neo-Confucian lecturer and acquaintance of Zhu, argued that the "Counsels of the Great Yu" passage reflected the influence of Laozi, the patriarch of Daoism, rather than Confucius. Lu maintained that the very idea of the mind-and-heart being split into adulterated and pure forms did not agree with the other ideas attributed to Confucius by his disciples. Lu did not reject the idea of principle; rather, he saw it simply as inherent in our functioning mind-and-heart (*xin*). He took the position that looking inward by "establishing the will" (or establishing resolve, *zhi*) would allow us to know principle without creating the epistemological dualism of somehow having two ways of knowing. His argument became an undercurrent that thereafter continued to tug at the ebb and flow of the tides of Neo-Confucianism.

Around 1500 Lu's position melded with Wang Yangming's Learning of the Mind-and-Heart school, which explicitly stated that principle was not to be sought in things but in one's own mind. While endorsing the recovery model that conceived of moral goodness as inherent in us at birth, Wang differed from Zhu Xi on the nature of knowledge. Access to innate goodness, Wang believed, did not come from the cumulative investigation of the many principles in external things. A moral value like filial piety was, after all, in one's mind-and-heart instead of in external things, so focusing on the mind-and-heart was the way to find principle. The charismatic teachings of Wang Yangming (often then called the Lu-Wang school) spread through popular assemblies and public meetings attended even by farmers, who were of quite a different background from the Song-period literati. Before long the court closed academies promoting this popular movement because it threatened to become an alternative center of authority to governmental power.

Neo-Confucianism as a label defines a cumulative tradition built upon principles that were new in the eleventh century. The tradition was more elastic than the dominant Cheng-Zhu Learning of the Way (Daoxue) faction, and the Lu-Wang faction singled itself out by its new epistemology. However, the Cheng-Zhu faction remained the dominant interpretation of Neo-Confucianism as later dynasties made it orthodoxy, and its self-cultivation methods sought to locate the patterns or principles that exist independently of human intentions or even consciousness. It declared that after true ethical classics had been composed in ancient China, all literate people were provided with a means of tapping into the principles of moral knowledge that are part of our human nature; and people of later eras could access those principles through the Four Books and the Five Classics. One consequence of this argument was that the culture that existed when the ancient classics were written did not itself have to be replicated, as long as the classics, as part of the process of self-cultivation, gave people access to the moral principles innate in each of us.

Newly Excavated Texts. Recently, a new archaeological dimension to arguments has emerged regarding the influence of Chinese Buddhism, with its Daoist assumptions, on Neo-Confucian philosophy. The excavation from 1973 to 1993 of several lost Confucian texts dating from the classical era supports the indigenous presence in the classical era of some Neo-Confucian ideas. These entombed texts corroborate the argument that in the late Warring States era Confucians described sages with access to atemporal natural patterns (*tiandao*) that could be parallel to the Neo-Confucian assumption of innate principles in human nature.

The director of the Institute of History at the Chinese Academy of Social Sciences in Beijing, Li Xueqin, argued in print from 1997 to 1999 that the excavated texts supported the claim that the *Great Learning* was written by Zengzi, the same senior disciple of Confucius whom Zhu Xi credits with authoring the *Great Learning* commentary. The institute director also claimed that the new texts confirmed that Zisi, Confucius' grandson, had authored the *Mean*. Both the *Great Learning* and the *Mean* were elevated to canonic status when Zhu included them among his Four Books in the founding of Neo-Confucianism.

It was Cheng Yi, a progenitor of Neo-Confucianism, who had argued that Zengzi alone stood out among the immediate disciples of Confucius and understood the inner meaning of the Master's message. Certain founders of Neo-Confucianism were made to look prescient by the excavated finds. Zhu Xi also celebrated the role of Zengzi in his preface to the *Great Learning* in the following way.

> No doubt, among the three thousand disciples of Confucius, none failed to hear his teachings, but it was only Zengzi who got the essential message and wrote this commentary to expound its meaning. Then, with the death of Mencius, the transmission vanished. This work [the *Great Learning*] survived, but few understood it. . . . The virtuous power of the Song Dynasty rose up, and both government and education shone with great luster, whereupon the two Cheng masters of Henan appeared and connected up with the tradition from Mencius [that had been long broken off]. The first truly to recognize and believe in this work, they expounded it to the world and further rearranged the fragmented text so as to bring out its essential message. With that, the method whereby the ancients taught men through the *Great Learning* with the guidance of the classic text of the Sage [Confucius] and the commentary of the Worthy [Zengzi], was once again made brilliantly clear to the world.[2]

Further, several scholars of the excavated texts believe today that some of the tomb findings can be attributed to the school of Zisi even though he may not have been the specific writer of those texts. One such text, titled *The Five Kinds of Action (Wuxing)*, now appears to be one of the earliest known Confucian works; it could date from just after the earliest chapters of the *Analects*. A tomb that was closed in 300 BCE contained a copy of *The Five Kinds of Action,* and there is now broad agreement that the text predates the life of Mencius. As late as the Northern Song there existed a collection of writings attributed to Zisi that may well have contained *The Five Kinds of Action*. The late-Qing scholar Huang Yizhou (1828–1899) has shown that this collection disappeared during the Southern Song when Zhu Xi lived.

The set of ancient texts excavated from 1973 to 1993 addressed the mind-and-heart (*xin*) as well as the qualities that are inherent in human nature at birth (*xing*), two subjects that were heavily empha-sized by the Song Neo-Confucians. This philosophically "inner" ori-entation was viewed in the eleventh century as a radical innovation in the thought of the Cheng brothers and later Zhu Xi, yet we now know it linked the brothers and Zhu with what appears to be one current of ideas in classical Confucian thought.

The following citation from *The Five Kinds of Action* connects not only to what Mencius would soon say in ancient China, but also to the similar points Neo-Confucians reasserted fifteen hundred years later. In these passages the encompassing fifth kind of action, sagacity, is not yet included in the discussion of the other four: humaneness, right-ness, ritual, and wisdom.

> [16.1] To see [the exemplary person's Way] and know it, is wisdom.
> To know it and be settled in it is humaneness.
> To be settled in it and apply it is rightness.
> To apply and show respect is ritual.
> [16.2] Humaneness and rightness are that from which ritual is born.
> [16.3] This is harmonizing of the four kinds of action.
> They harmonize and then they are made the same.
> They are made the same and then there is goodness.[3]

The parallel later is clear. In the opening sentences of the preface to the *Great Learning* Zhu Xi cites Mencius, noting, "When Heaven gives birth to the people, it gives each one, without exception, a nature of humaneness, rightness, ritual, and wisdom."

While there is still no conclusive proof that Zengzi wrote the commentary to the *Great Learning,* three key ideas in the *Great Learning* — cultivating one's person (*xiu shen*), renewing the people (*xin min*), and vigilant solitariness (*shen du*) — also appear in the texts excavated from the two tombs between 1973 and 1993 and are now commonly attributed by scholars to Zengzi's student, Zisi. Given the Neo-Confucian focus on the *Great Learning,* the *Mencius,* and the *Mean,* it is not surprising that the new texts have stimulated renewed discussion and affirmation of the indigenous origins of some Neo-Confucian ideas.

These textual finds from classical China do not by themselves eliminate the possibility of Buddhist and Daoist influences on either the metaphysics or the epistemology of Neo-Confucians. However, the attribution of universals singled out by early Neo-Confucians to classical Confucian texts, and then the discovery of those ideas described as innate in newly excavated classical texts, raises the question of the indigenous origins of Neo-Confucian ideas to be further explored by future scholarship and perhaps future excavation.

Self-Cultivation

The third trait defining Neo-Confucianism is an elaborated program for self-cultivation. The *Mencius* text, established by Zhu Xi as one of the Four Books, claimed that inherent in human nature are the sprouts, or capacities, to develop into four lived moral values: humaneness, rightness, ritual, and wisdom. But Zhu reread Mencius in his own way. Instead of a developmental model in which nurturing is necessary to make sprouts grow, Zhu claimed our "original nature" could release these same moral values or principles if the material force in which they were embedded could be refined in each of us. Self-cultivation through moral learning consistently clarifies the material force, *qi,* in which are embedded all principles of our original nature. Principle then can start to shine through our material nature.

The human capacity to transform our physical nature in this way is not shared by, for example, dogs or horses. Horses, bees, and other animals reflecting social behavior were considered by Zhu to have the same principle in their natures, but they were also assumed to have no way to refine the physical matter obscuring and blocking it. Without self-cultivation to refine their *qi,* other animals, unlike humans, are unable to reveal principle in their natural endowment.

Once we actually recognize principle in ourselves, Zhu felt, we also activate that moral principle in our behavior. Zhu composed his own chapter of commentary explaining the recognition (or investigation) of things (*ge wu*) in the *Great Learning,* and that explanation became the starting point for the Eight-Step path of development for the morally exemplary person. These sophisticated steps to self-cultivation went beyond intellectual mastery of texts to include demonstrable changes in conduct and became a lasting legacy of Song Confucian thought. Even Qing dynasty Confucians (writing in the period from 1700 to 1900) who did not accept humaneness and goodness as ready-made in human nature still relied upon active training in self-cultivation to create personal actions that would build these qualities into our conduct.

Living with reverence for one another is essential to living a life of self-cultivation. Huang Gan (1152–1221), the disciple and son-in-law of Zhu Xi, stated that "abiding in reverence" was the basis of all self-cultivation. To Neo-Confucians the core meaning of reverence (*jing*) was single-mindedness, but it was easily generalized to mean moral seriousness, or what is inside us that allows respect to be expressed externally to others.

It should be noted that transformation through reverent interpersonal relationships extended explicit references to self-cultivation by other simple techniques in the passages of the *Analects*. Ritual, for example, had long been a key to self-cultivation among the immediate disciples of Confucius. The archaic written character that denoted ritual, or ritual propriety, *li* (禮), suggested what ancient shamans assumed to be a one-to-one response from the spirits in their religious ceremonies: an offering is over a fire, and on the left is the radical (or meaning unit) for spirits. But the meaning of the ceremonial word was clearly moral by the time Confucius used it, as any spirits and ghosts were kept at a distance in early Confucian teaching. The deep respect or reverence needed during the ceremony, for example, of an ancestral sacrifice became a virtue in itself. As Confucius worded it, "What could I see in a person who . . . in observing ritual propriety is not respectful, and who in overseeing the mourning rites does not grieve?" (*Analects* 3.26). The key to making rituals function effectively was always the presence of voluntary, self-generated respect. To the question "As for the young contributing their energies when there is work to be done, and deferring to their elders when there is wine and food to be had — how can merely doing this be considered filial?" came the answer from the Master: "It all lies in showing the proper countenance (*Analects* 2.8)."

As a kind of case study, Neo-Confucians analyzed the incomplete journey toward sagehood of the Master's favorite student in the *Analects*. It was clear that Hui (pronounced "whey") had not gotten as far as he could have on his moral quest, yet he had been so promising that his premature death left Confucius distraught for over a year. One way that Neo-Confucians explained the student's shortcoming was that, unlike Confucius, Hui had relied too heavily on external techniques of self-cultivation. What was missing, the Neo-Confucians assumed, was "getting it oneself" (*zide*); that is, Hui exhibited model behavior when among others, but he had not fully internalized the transformative power of moral values so that he could continue to develop spiritually.

The Neo-Confucians believed that self-cultivation should access one's inner moral potential. Zhu Xi combined the exhaustive search for that potential with abiding in reverence in one's relationships, and the most efficient way to recognize moral principle was serious study of the reshaped canon of classics. Reverential relationships and extracting moral principle from the classics defined a two-pronged program for self-cultivation, and the focus of both practices was the internalization of one's increasing moral knowledge so it would be naturally externalized in one's renewed behavior. This form of self-cultivation was preserved as the basic insight of Song Neo-Confucianism — even after nineteenth-century Confucians no longer highlighted the Neo-Confucian doctrine of metaphysical principles. As the program of self-cultivation is an essential component of Neo-Confucianism with a lasting legacy, it is the basic theme of the middle chapters of this book.

Song-period Neo-Confucians agreed that self-cultivation was essential to leading a moral life. Our moral action springs from a mind-and-heart that is clearly aware of principle. Moral principle itself is directly accessible from the lessons of the ancient sages and ethical worthies who composed the Four Books, and that study was one fundamental way to self-cultivate. The process of learning, however, should also connect everyday behavior to our innate goodness. Thus moral principle should also come through contact with the practical affairs of the world, and most immediately through respectful interaction with other people. Realizing our moral potential as human beings means treating others humanely, doing what is morally appropriate, conducting relationships with the reverence of ritual propriety, and acting with the wisdom that distinguishes right from wrong. The lifelong program of learning to realize this human potential begins and ends with a systematic program of Neo-Confucian education, which is the subject of the next chapter.

CHAPTER 2

Neo-Confucian Education

Of the three components defining Neo-Confucianism (see chapter 1), self-cultivation and the reshaped canon of classics were more lasting than the metaphysical and epistemological content of the philosophical doctrine. At the end of the nineteenth century, for example, the revision of the Song dynasty doctrine made the metaphysics of "principle" and the aim of all individuals to become sages dispensable. Systematic moral self-cultivation, however, remained indispensable.

The importance of the role of self-cultivation in attaining a moral life owed much to the emphasis on this idea in Neo-Confucian academies. By the end of the Song period in 1279 some sixty Neo-Confucian academies throughout China trained the insights of the Cheng brothers and Zhu Xi into graduating classes each year. These graduates in turn would go on to found more academies, and they all contributed to Zhu's personal aim of creating a dual system of higher education apart from the state's vocational interests. Without new forms of education perpetuating Neo-Confucianism, the Song-era Cheng-Zhu school of thought would have been less important in Chinese history.

Beginning from the twelfth century, the most sophisticated Confucian academies, each with a headmaster and anywhere between twenty-five and three hundred students, perfected a system of training young men in the mastery of an established corpus of philosophical and historical texts. This was higher education in the Neo-Confucian paradigm, and while academy objectives did not forbid students from taking the dynastic civil service examination, Zhu refused to allow training for governmental examinations in those academies he personally founded because he believed the study of the humanities should ideally remain independent of job seeking. The academy-educated typically found jobs on the staffs of high officials or as local clerks; others were hired to serve the needs of local communities in clan schools or private libraries, or in editing local genealogical records for well-established families. Like the Five Masters of the Northern Song, the headmasters of these Neo-Confucian academies committed their professions quite consciously to scholarship, as opposed to official careers. And many aspects of the humanistic education provided in these institutions would be the envy today of the best liberal arts institutions in the United States.

For example, the White Deer Grotto Academy established a set of pedagogical precepts under Zhu Xi's guidance that appeared again and again in the founding documents of new academies all the way into the nineteenth century. While in residence on the academy's campus, students were to conduct themselves respectfully according to these precepts: "(a) When in your conduct you are unable to succeed, reflect and look [for the cause] within yourself; (b) Do not do to others what you would not want them to do to you; (c) Curb your anger and restrain your lust; turn to the good and correct your errors; and (d) Be faithful and true to your words and firm and sincere in conduct."[1]

The curriculum and pedagogy at good Confucian academies — up to the end of the nineteenth century — were smoothly coordinated and usually two-pronged: first, essay examinations were given at the end of each month, and second, students kept daily notebooks of their personal reactions to their readings. The latter practice began in the Song-period academies; later Confucian academies, which often were founded explicitly with Song-era academy precepts as their guide, taught the student that what he took away as a passage's meaning should constitute the content of his daily notebook of reactions to the classical texts.

At academies such as these there was space for tutorials on each campus, as well as a lecture hall for talks by master scholars, but there were no small-group classrooms. As this pedagogy implied by lectures paired with personal tutorials was perfected, the headmaster conducted a tutorial meeting with a student as often as every five days; this tutorial centered on the student's personal notebook of glosses explaining passages, which was presented to the headmaster for his careful criticism.

The addition of student notebooks in conjunction with tutorials was not happenstance; the pedagogy of Confucian academies fit with the compilation of experientially based sayings that made up texts like the *Analects*. Neo-Confucians such as Zhu Xi felt that the most productive way to read the collected sayings of Confucius and his disciples was to begin with those the student believed addressed issues relevant in his own life. With the assistance of perceptive philosophical commentaries on passages, usually presented in an interlinear fashion within the classic text, and relying upon the experience of the individual reader to give them meaning, students read the brief passages until some insight spoke to them, and that would trigger an entry in their personal notebooks.

Neo-Confucian academy pedagogy was intentionally designed to focus the students' learning much less on the teacher's knowledge and more on the students' interaction with the classical texts. In other words, Confucius, Zengzi and Zisi (the assumed authors of the *Great Learning* and the *Mean,* respectively), Mencius, and Yan Hui — the latter the most accomplished disciple in the *Analects* — were the real teachers. Following several years of basic schooling, the (roughly) three years a student typically spent at a Confucian academy should have allowed him to find his own moral voice. This voice became his own through the combination of study and interpersonal practice. Each student in an academy took his stand in tutorials and on essay questions so regularly that all students had ample training in how to continue as independent learners for life.

There are good records of the teaching at a Neo-Confucian academy run by a man who was a close friend of Zhu Xi. These records reveal that one divisive issue was how to maintain a balance between textual study and one's interpersonal ethical practice. Lü Zuqian, Zhu's collaborator in composing *Reflections on Things at Hand,* the anthology of Neo-Confucian thinkers, was perhaps the most famous Neo-Confucian teacher of their era during the Song dynasty. Lü, a reformer, ran his own very popular Beautiful Pools Academy in the center of what is now the southeastern province of Zhejiang. He argued at the time that teachers in many academies had no right to complain about poor social customs because by not adequately training their students to change such customs, they ultimately were responsible for them. He elaborated that teachers should guide their students to avoid the hazardous tendency toward scholasticism. Lü once wrote to Zhu,

> Extending knowledge and energetically practicing are interconnected and mutually reinforcing. If students have solid intentions, then teaching, pondering, searching, and concentrating certainly

are the essentials for advancing in virtue. There are some among the younger generation who expend much effort on seeking the meaning of words but little on daily practice and experience. Although they may achieve some vague understanding, they actually have nothing to apply to themselves. . . . I am not saying to have them practice with vigor and slow down their extension of knowledge, but the one directing them should have an orderly procedure.[2]

Some three hundred students at a time attended Lü's academy. He asked students to keep notebooks of the doubts that emerged from their readings, to meet in small groups to discuss these doubts, and to relate the content of their readings to contemporary problems. They signed each other's notebooks to flag which issues had been discussed, and submitted these records to the headmaster.

Zhu criticized Lü for including civil service exam preparation every ten days at his academy. For Zhu the study of the humanities should ideally remain independent of job seeking. Education was for the personal development of the individual. While the court did come to financially support Neo-Confucian academies in the Song period, the court did not succeed in manipulating their curriculum or the pedagogy to serve state vocational goals.

Self-Cultivation in Neo-Confucian Education

Age-Specific Educational Norms

Mongol conquerors defeated the Song dynasty in 1279, but since they had no tradition of bureaucratic recruitment, they chose to rely upon the Song civil service examination system to recruit the staff of the Yuan dynasty government bureaucracy. Neo-Confucian education was defined by a graduated schedule of reading in certain texts, and this was taught within the Neo-Confucian academy curriculum. One master teacher in the Yuan dynasty, Cheng Duanli, enshrined this age-specific curriculum in a "Daily Schedule of Study" with a variety of charts attached to use for checking off one's progress.

In a typical educated family, by age five a son would have begun the recitation by heart of the three major literacy primers: *Three Character Classic, Hundred Family Names,* and *Thousand Character Classic.* The objective was to master the two thousand or so characters included in the primers as a rudimentary form of literacy. Reciting the *Three Character Classic* first initiated mastery of Neo-Confucian ideas, which can be detected in the opening of the text.

> Human beings at birth / Are naturally good.
> Their natures are much the same / [But] nurture takes them far apart.
> If there is not teaching / The nature will deteriorate
> The right way in teaching / Is to value concentration.
> To feed the body and not the mind / Would be the father's fault.
> Instruction without discipline / Is sloth on the teacher's part. . . .[3]

Thus continues the passages for 356 lines of three characters each, which rhyme every other line, and by the end contain about 500 different characters.

Next came the *Hundred Family Names,* believed to have been composed during the Northern Song period, and which simply arranged the most common family names in 118 lines of four characters each. Capping off this basic lesson in literacy was the *Thousand Character Classic,* which also rhymed lines alternatively, with four characters in each line. Rhyming facilitated the process of memorization, an essential tool for a young man ultimately moving toward the national civil service examinations. During the Yuan dynasty educators recommended an explicitly Neo-Confucian text titled *The Primer on Human Nature and Principle* to replace the *Thousand Character Classic,* as it more systematically introduced Neo-Confucian thought.

Before young sons began formal schooling with oral recitation of the classics (around age eight), they were required to study *Elementary Learning,* a textbook compiled by Zhu Xi. Classical Confucianism emphasized a prescribed set of social obligations that were the core of ethical training, and these obligations remained basic to the social structure in Neo-Confucian education. The five foundational relationships were defined as parent-child, ruler-minister, husband-wife, elder-younger, and friend-friend. The young student found the central ideas of Zhu's *Elementary Learning* to consist of quotations from classical texts that focused on the development of the five relationships; other passages treated basic standards of etiquette and personal conduct. At the same time, education at home reinforced a set of respectful kinship terms that socialized the student in the correct use of different terms of address for relatives according to the genealogical distance of the relative from one's parents. The deference and duties attached to each social role were reciprocal and implied moral obligations from both parties, not just the younger person.

From age eight to fifteen a student following Neo-Confucian education would enter family, clan, or public schools, which introduced the first set of classics to the curriculum: (1) the Five Classics (without commentary explaining the passages), along with (2) the newly distinguished set of Four Books (also without commentaries). The nine texts comprised more than four hundred thousand characters that had to be committed to memory in order. The method of instruction involved reading aloud each section of a text one hundred times, followed by oral recitation of the same section from memory one hundred times. Once a section of text was memorized, the student moved to another section. The teacher conducted regular testing of larger portions of the text — perhaps an entire chapter, for example. The curriculum was so rigorous that only the brightest and most determined students completed it successfully.

After completing the first stage of formal schooling, students moved on to the next level, the period from age fifteen to twenty-two, which required new texts, less memorization, and more reflection and analysis. These older students were asked to refer to the Neo-Confucian anthology *Reflections on Things at Hand,* which is filled with brilliant selections from the Five Masters of the Northern Song in which provocative metaphors opened avenues into the interior life of the student.

Zhu Xi's substantive commentaries on the expanded Neo-Confucian canon of classics defined human psychology as read through Zhu's interpretation of the passages. During this second period of formal study students sought an in-depth understanding of what at age eight was largely a mastering of words in order. The memorized passages from childhood would light up with meaning as a student's life experience provided the filaments to make them comprehensible. At this time each student would also single out one of the Five Classics for further specialized study. The curriculum further included a comprehensive history, as well as a set of model readings to improve one's writing style. Finally, a poetry text, *Chu Songs,* again including Zhu's commentary, completed this advanced phase of education.

How to Study a Classic

In 1190 Zhu Xi, as editor of the first edition of the Four Books, expressed his deep concern that students would read the new compilation superficially. Knowing the deleterious effects of memorizing texts for the national civil service examinations, which caused students to neglect a personal understanding of the classics, Zhu worried that even academy students would develop superficial reading habits in their anxiety to pass the examinations. Exacerbating the problem was the fact that woodblock printings of the older canon of the Confucian classics (available by 932 CE) made the Four Books more readily available to students, thus rendering obsolete the practice of meticulously recopying the books in order to possess one's own copies. Zhu complained, "Because nowadays the number of printed texts is so large, people don't put their minds to reading them. . . . For people today even copying down a text has become bothersome. Therefore their reading is sloppy. When students today read a text, it's just as if they had never read it. When they haven't read it, it's just as if they had."

In particular, Zhu complained that oral recitation of texts was being sacrificed. He commented, "It would seem that the ancients had no written texts, so only if they had memorized a work from beginning to end would they get it. Those studying a text would memorize it completely, and afterward receive instruction on it from a teacher." Zhu feared that by no longer committing the text to memory, students would have a weaker grasp of the meaning of the argument. He continued, "The method of reading is to recite a text, then ponder it over; to ponder it over; then recite it. Oral recitation of a text helps us to think about it. For our minds then hover over the words."[4]

Careless reading habits needed critical examination before one picked up an ethical classic. Zhu felt that readers commonly imposed on texts a practice akin to finishing a sentence for someone in conversation: such an interruption represented a gross discourtesy to the speaker and revealed an inability to listen. Zhu argued that readers practiced this discourtesy against themselves in reading great texts. If a classic is subtle enough to contain moral messages worth finding, then the reader cannot jump to conclusions part way through a paragraph. By assuming ahead of time what the point would be, a reader was being discourteous to the sagacious words of the classic. Reading in such a manner would be worse than cutting off a friend's sentence, for one had everything to benefit from not cutting off the sages and moral worthies who authored the text.

In other words, we should have an open mind as we read the wisdom in an ethical classic. If we can empty our minds of what we think it will say, and calm ourselves to be as placid as a serene pond, then we will have a reasonable chance to receive and reflect accurately the ideas in the text. Single-minded concentration on the words will help. Zhu advised sitting comfortably at a table and humming gently to truly clear one's mind before opening a classic.

Zhu believed that an appropriate metaphor for the process of reading was correctly watering a garden. Growth cannot be rushed; oversaturation can impede or halt growth. This metaphor brings to mind the related story that Mencius had heard in ancient times: a farmer wanted to help his grain grow, so one day he proudly reported to his family that he had exhausted himself by pulling up a little higher every sprout in the field. His son hurried out to look, only to find wilted sprouts everywhere. Likewise, speed reading can be self-defeating. By slowing down and not progressing to harder material until the preceding texts have been fully understood, Zhu felt a reader had a better chance to internalize the moral message. And naturally the same principle would apply in one's actions — Zhu noted that an occasional good deed was not the equivalent to treating everyone with an inner sense of rightness.

As a teacher, Zhu informed his students that reading for personal growth should occupy 70 percent of one's total reading, thus leaving only 30 percent for examination and career preparation. By reading for the self and not others, one could regain control of what to read and become more autonomous in the practice of lifelong learning. Confucius, too, had complained about the same problem during his time: "Scholars of old would study for their own sake, while those of today do so to impress others" (*Analects* 14.24).

Zhu's *dushufa,* or advice on reading, addressed how best to make use of existing commentaries on the classics. In his view, a careful reading of the text of a classic at least, say, ten times should yield 40 or 50 percent of the meaning of the passages. Referring to the established commentaries of past scholars could add as much as 30 percent more to the student's understanding. It then remained up to the student to reread the text until the final 20 percent or so was completely understood.

For Zhu the first rule in reading responsibly was to allow one's rate of comprehension to determine one's speed of reading. He warned, "Students nowadays don't think about their own strength when reading. I fear that we are not able to handle the reading we set out for ourselves." He strongly advised reading a small amount and completely understanding it before moving ahead to study new material, or a second book. He again compared this to organic growth from the soil: studying for self-cultivation required respecting the stages of tilling the ground, fertilizing, planting the seed, watering, and weeding, as one would on the land.

Further, concentrating on the meaning and sound of a passage as one memorizes it is a way to correct thoughtless reading. Many classics were in fact written with mnemonic devices built into their phrasing for easy memorization, and the ability to recite a passage allowed the learner to ponder the passage at any time of the day, in any place. For example, in the *Great Learning* the predicate of one sentence, or clause, often becomes the subject of the next, as in "Things being recognized, knowing can be extended; knowing being extended, the intentions can be made sincere." Once memorized, the relevant text could be pulled up when the student was ready to apply those ideas.

The second rule of responsible reading was that careful readers had to be constantly alert to not impose their own ideas onto the text. Readers "mustn't come to it [the text] with their own ideas about what it will say," Zhu wrote, and in a letter to a friend he is explicit about why this is so important: "One cannot first fix your opinion" of what the text says; otherwise, "you cannot see the original meaning intended by the sages and worthies."

Once a learner begins reading, that person maintains an even temperament that will allow consistently objective reading. Based on a common Neo-Confucian metaphor that had its origins in the Daoist thinker Zhuangzi, the idea was to polish and uncloud the mirror of the mind so that the meaning of the text could be accurately reflected. Maintaining objectivity required mental training to remain even-tempered and not prejudge the meaning of a passage.

Third, a student had to maintain single-minded concentration on the text. Correct reading and study techniques had a lasting influence as a component of one's personal self-cultivation. At a point where students of other religious traditions might look toward joining the priesthood or a monastery, a Confucian student took responsibility for his or her personal spiritual practice through systematic study. For the serious student, the repeated study of a passage while integrating the analysis of established commentaries meant spending the better part of a decade on mastering the Four Books. Finally, like the recommended sequence of studying the Four Books, the student should maintain a sequential order in his (or her) reading so that depth of understanding could become progressively greater.

Zhu Xi on the *Analects*

One important reason that Zhu Xi assembled the relatively short Four Books as additions to the old canon of the Five Classics was his perception that earlier education in the Confucian tradition had not sufficiently stressed the inherent goodness of human nature. As we have seen, Zhu touted Zengzi, Confucius' senior disciple, as a spokesperson for this viewpoint. But in reading his own understanding into the few recorded words of Zengzi in the *Analects,* Zhu radically revised earlier commentaries to bring them into accord with what he felt had previously been neglected in understanding this early text.

In *Analects* 1.4, for example, Zhu added his own interpretation to Zengzi's three criteria for daily self-examination. Zengzi said, "Every day I examine my own person on three counts: in working on behalf of others, have I failed to be true to myself? In my associations with friends, have I failed to be true to my word? As for what has been passed on to me, have I failed to rehearse it?"[5] Earlier commentaries interpreted the passage as placing less emphasis on the inner impulse for one's behavior, as Zhu did, than on the responsibility one has to others before passing along something one may not have practiced in oneself. Zhu insisted that the passage laid out a three-step sequence that progressed from (1) revealing one's mind-and-heart to (2) subsequently confirming what is revealed in one's mind to (3) the preceding steps becoming the basis of what one's teacher has passed along.

In Zhu's reconstruction, Zengzi appears to be an advocate for exposing and expressing the nature of one's mind as it is, in all its natural goodness. In Zhu's influential reorganization of the *Great Learning,* as well, Zengzi is firmly asserted to be the original author of the ten chapters of commentary accompanying the simple seven-paragraph text attributed to Confucius. Zhu's interpretation of "revealing" one's inner nature found in Zengzi's commentary was a fundamental shift in understanding the text itself, and it started students off on their long journeys toward inner self-cultivation. Zhu left the reader with the conviction that revealing one's inner nature was implicitly at the heart of self-cultivation in the classical period. This was one reason Zhu worked on the analysis of this text and Zengzi's commentary until the last days of his life. He was so effective and influential that the older, less inner-directed and more socially directed reading of the *Great Learning* would not reassert itself in commentaries for several hundred years.

In Zhu's judgment, Zengzi had achieved the condition of only partially identifying with humaneness despite his inner-directed orientation. Such a state was *zhong* (to reveal one's mind fully), but not yet a state of *ren* (humaneness). Zhu assumed that Zengzi, as advanced as his learning was, had not reached a consistent state of humaneness on par with Confucius. If Zengzi had continued his three-step practice of self-cultivation longer, then he would have fully perceived the interconnectedness of the different moral dispositions inherent in human nature and thus would have attained humaneness.

There are also two lines in *Analects* 6.30 that Zhu treated as defining the kind of advanced self-cultivation in which humaneness is firmly rooted in a person. The end of the passage reads, "Now wishing himself to be established, the humane person establishes others; and wishing himself to achieve prominence, the humane person makes others prominent. The ability to draw analogies from what is near at hand can be called the way to humaneness." The last line, Zhu believed, referred to the methodical work on the Confucian Golden Rule: "Do not do unto others what you would not want done to yourself." In other words, readers applying this idea to their relationships in any era would use the analogy of what we would not want done to us to determine the moral course of action in an ethical situation.

Zhu assumed that there was more to the advanced level of truly humane interaction that was not self-referential. To wit, all later readers would then know that when we are intuitively in touch with the state of humaneness, then we understand the substance of the principle of goodness endowed in us at birth. In such a state of moral perfection, we can establish others and work for the prominence of others as quickly and reflexively as we can do those same things for ourselves. Such a state would be the result of a sophisticated and sustained development of self-cultivation that accesses a deep understanding of how morality works in all of human nature. Fully realized humaneness, besides placing others first, can even connect us to how this inherent principle works in the natural world beyond human interaction. Neo-Confucians such as Zhang Zai wrote text like the "Western Inscription," which developed this connection, and this idea will be treated later in this book.

Nevertheless, the conscious self-discipline with which Zengzi in ancient times did succeed in working on himself had, Zhu felt, made it possible for him alone, among all the disciples of Confucius, to see the underlying relationship between revealing one's mind fully (*zhong*) and being able to infer from one's innate endowment of goodness to extend that goodness (*shu*) to others. In *Analects* 4.15 Zengzi is said to have understood the subtle relationship between recognizing the nature of one's inner mind and extending it outward to others, hence he at least had a clear glimpse of what humaneness could be and how it functioned in one's relationships. But a sage such as Confucius went well beyond referring back to self-interest to determine how to act morally. And the fact that Zengzi wrote a commentary on the *Great Learning* highlighted that work as a key to Zengzi's own significant achievement in self-cultivation.

Neo-Confucian Education and Women

Neo-Confucian thought and practice have been accused of contributing to women's declining position after its formulation. Discussion of the gendered social norms in the Song period will contextualize what Neo-Confucians wrote regarding the family and its proper social norms. In elite society during the Song dynasty, women's activities typically focused on the family, with female duties after marriage centering on perpetuating the patrilineal succession of the husband's family. Such duties entailed childbearing and child rearing, including bearing primary responsibility for the children's early education. Teaching her children the rudiments of literacy and ensuring that tutors were available thereafter meant a wife in an elite family needed to possess at least basic skills in literacy. Zhu Xi conceived of a male social role in the family that did not include household money management or careful attention to household affairs. The duties of a good wife entailed caring for her husband's living parents as if they were her own, as well as household management — which included household finances.

The rights and responsibilities surrounding dowries and concubines complicated conflicts over family property in the increasingly commercialized Song era. Neo-Confucian scholars addressed family customs in ways that revealed their primary concern with maintaining order in family lines of succession. Sima Guang's (1019–1086) work on rituals contributed to Zhu's arguments in the latter's influential manual titled *Family Rituals (Jiali)*. Descriptions of coming-of-age initiations, weddings, funerals, and sacrifices to ancestors were all gendered, and males were consistently placed in positions of authority. The cult of female chastity both before marriage and after the death of a husband grew for a variety of reasons in the Song period. And many scholars opposed the remarriage of widows in order to keep the family system of property inheritance in the patriline and at the same time not to confuse filial piety. Redefining the family unit would raise difficult questions: if a widow remarried, was an existing son to switch his filial devotion to the ancestral line of the nonbiological father? Or should his devotion and inheritance remain tied to the family of his biological father, even though his mother had left? Did the family obligations of a married woman to her mother-in-law end with the death of her husband? Despite such questions, it was nevertheless common in the Song period for widows to remarry. Overall it is true that Neo-Confucian scholars contributed to the sharpening hierarchical social rules for women — their motivation being a desire to maintain social order through male-dominated hierarchies within the family system.

Zhu personally saw the Song state in a tense cold war. The Jurchen had occupied the Northern Song capital just before his birth and demanded formal Chinese surrender of northern prefectures to permanent Jurchen control. In this time of crisis it was natural for him to assume that strong families with traditional gender roles were a bulwark of moral strength. The seventeen funerary inscriptions that

Zhu composed in memory of women during the Song period reflected one such traditional gender role for them: the success of the mother's sons was clearly regarded as the ultimate test of the mother's virtue, modeling, and competence.

Neo-Confucian gender assumptions continued into the Ming period (1368–1644). During the Ming dynasty, however, the Four Books for Women were published, composed of works written by and for women. It is not known who compiled these four works, but the component books are *Admonitions for Women,* written in the Han period and composed by Ban Zhao (ca. 48–ca. 116); the *Analects for Women* by Song Ruozhao, who had been appointed as a scholar at the court of the Dezong emperor in the Tang dynasty (r. 780–805); the *Classic of Filiality for Women,* written by Madam Cheng, the wife of a Tang-period official named Chen Miao; and the impressive *Instructions for the Inner Quarters* by Empress Xu, the wife of the Yongle emperor of the Ming dynasty (r. 1402–1424).

Empress Xu credited Empress Ma, the wife of the founding Ming emperor, with the content of *Instructions for the Inner Quarters,* which she had received in person from Empress Ma early in her married life, before her husband became the third emperor of the Ming. The *Instructions* went well beyond the conventional views of women's roles in the home at the time; indeed, they parallel Zhu's *Elementary Learning,* except addressed to women. One impressive aspect of this book is that Empress Xu clearly assumed women were as capable of achieving morally exemplary behavior and sagehood as men, despite the disadvantages created by little or no opportunity for systematic instruction. Empress Xu made Neo-Confucian assumptions regarding innate endowment and tailored the process of self-cultivation for women as follows.

For a person to master sagehood, nothing is more crucial than nourishing one's moral nature so that one is able to cultivate one's self. . . . Being upright and modest, reserved and quiet, correct and dignified, sincere and honest: these constitute the moral nature of a woman. Being filial and respectful, humane and perspicacious, loving and warm, meek and gentle: these represent the complete development of the moral nature. The moral nature being innate in our endowment, it becomes transformed and fulfilled through practice. It is not something that comes from outside but is actually rooted in our very selves.[6]

To conclude this chapter on Neo-Confucian education, an explanation of the custom of the funerary inscriptions (*muzhiming*), which scholars wrote for their peers and students wrote for their teachers, will underline the important teacher-student relationship in Neo-Confucianism. Such inscriptions were longer than obituaries and were generally much warmer and more personal in tone. They testified to a remarkable collegiality in the lifelong pursuit of learning that many scholars shared and often contained personal testimonials from younger scholars regarding the lasting influence of the deceased on their lives.

The heartfelt bond between student and teacher stands out in these testimonials, which fill the many printed histories of Confucian scholars in different dynasties; the funerary inscriptions were also sometimes carved into stone steles. Apart from filial devotion to one's family, it is clear that the lifelong debt of many Neo-Confucian students to their teachers was transformative in their lives. The teachers discussed in many of the testimonials may not have been prominent enough to have biographies in the official dynastic histories, but the existence of hundreds of volumes of scholarly lineages and published funerary inscriptions is evidence of the impact their lives and work had on students. It is abundantly clear that many literati indeed practiced the spirit of the humane Neo-Confucian ideal that became an educational model from the Song era into the nineteenth century.

PART II

The *Great Learning* and the Eight Steps to Personal Cultivation

CHAPTER 3

The First Five Steps of Personal Cultivation

The Confucian Eight Steps are embedded in a remarkably short, one-page classic, the *Great Learning*. In the 1100s CE this ancient text was singled out from among the ritual texts compiled during the Han dynasty as the cardinal work with which to begin one's adult education in Confucian ethics. The brief paragraphs of the *Great Learning* are a framework on which students can flesh out the moral path to humaneness. Anyone, not just eminent scholars or chosen disciples, can enter the gateway to sagehood by studying and applying to their lives the steps in this classic. The most prominent Confucians in China, as well as in Chosŏn-era Korea (1392–1910 CE) and Tokugawa Japan (1603–1868 CE), understood and promoted the central importance of the *Great Learning* in the process of self-cultivation.

The middle of the brief text contains the Eight Steps that make up the core of self-cultivation and that make the connection between individual self-cultivation and civil conduct in the social and political order. During the 800s Confucians in China perceived this important insight in the text, and the bridge linking private internal growth with public social order became crucial in Neo-Confucian thought in the eleventh century. The complete text of the *Great Learning* can be broken into discrete paragraphs as follows, with paragraphs four and five containing the Eight Steps.[1]

One remarkable feature of this work is the fact that so many later Confucians felt it could connect any historical age to the lost or hidden insights of the ancient Confucian classics. By following the leading Neo-Confucian interpretations of the personal phase of the Eight Steps, this chapter will explore how those steps might apply to later periods, including the present. The explanations of how each step works are from Song-period Neo-Confucians.

The *Great Learning*

1. The way of the *Great Learning* lies in clearly manifesting luminous virtue, renewing the people, and resting in the utmost good.
2. Knowing where to rest, there is stability; with stability, one can have composure; with composure one can be at peace; at peace one can reflect, and with reflection one can get there.
3. Things have their roots and branches. Affairs have a beginning and an end. Knowing what comes before and what comes after is close to the Way.
4. The ancients, wishing clearly to manifest luminous virtue to all-under-Heaven, first put in order their own states. Wishing to govern their states, they first regulated their families. Wishing to regulate their families, they first cultivated their own persons. Wishing to cultivate their persons, they first rectified their minds-and-hearts [*xin*]. Wishing to rectify their minds-and-hearts, they first made their intentions sincere. Wishing to make their intentions sincere, they first extended their knowing. The extension of knowing lies in recognizing [investigating] things and affairs.
5. Things being recognized, knowing can be extended; knowing being extended, the intentions can be made sincere; the intentions being made sincere, the mind-and-heart can be rectified; the mind-and-heart rectified, the person can be cultivated; with the person cultivated, the family can be regulated; the family regulated, the state can be governed; the state governed, all-under-Heaven can be at peace.
6. From the Son of Heaven down to the common people, they all as one take cultivating the person to be the root.
7. How could it be that the root be disturbed and yet have the branch remain undisturbed? Never should the important be treated as trivial; never should the trivial be treated as important.

Neo-Confucian students were taught that in ancient times, when the sage-kings no longer ruled the earliest states, both popular custom and education deteriorated. Zhu Xi reconstructed what happened next in his preface to the *Great Learning* in 1189.

> At that time the sage Confucius appeared, but being unable to attain the position of ruler-teacher by which to carry out government and education, he could do no more than recite the ways of the sage kings and pass them along, in order to make them known to later generations. . . . There was, however, this piece, the *Great Learning,* which followed up what had been accomplished in elementary learning with a view to setting forth the lucid teaching methods of the higher learning. Thus for outward emulation there would be a model great enough to serve as the highest standard of perfection, and for inner cultivation something detailed enough to spell out in full its sequence and contents.[2]

Confucius was an extremely perceptive observer of human nature. He assumed, for example, that both within and beyond the social unit of the family, "making good on your word and doing your utmost in relationships" helped build the moral values of each person. As this mindset is described in the *Analects,* "The Master said, 'I am not sure that anyone who does not make good on their word is viable as a person. If a large carriage does not have the pin for its yoke, or a small carriage does not have the pin for its crossbar, how can you drive them anywhere?'" (2.22). Self-cultivation builds humaneness by being trustworthy in what one says and in practicing thoughtfulness about the interests of others, which means internalizing responsibility for the effects of one's behavior on others.

When relationships are conducted by people who have cultivated themselves, those relationships become the medium for the extension and development of the humaneness of each person. One's capacity to be humane increases like the rings of a tree as one repeatedly conducts relationships with deep respect or reverence. The *Reflections on Things at Hand* anthology suggests that a couple of years of living with a calm, self-cultivated mind will naturally foster one's upright behavior, so one's mind-and-heart will be "rectified" (*Reflections* IV.67) — that is, become intentionally caring and unbiased. The work of increasing hu-

maneness will ideally reach a point of internalized humaneness identifying with one's innate character. Confucius himself appears not only
to have reached this advanced moral state of self-cultivation, but also
become one with it at the age of seventy. He stated that at that point he
could "follow the desires of my mind-and-heart without overstepping
[right]" (Watson, *Analects* 2.4).

The Eight-Step program is a straightforward means to show that
self-cultivation can connect to the promise of community harmony
and even peace among communities or among nations. Because self-
cultivation is lifelong, these steps define not a political structure, but
a practice to be socialized into the ruled and rulers alike. The Eight
Steps are as follows:

1. Recognize (or Investigate) Things and Affairs
2. Extend One's Knowing
3. Make One's Intentions Sincere
4. Rectify One's Mind
5. Cultivate the Person
6. Regulate the Family
7. Order the State
8. Bring Peace to All

Their objective, as understood by Zhu Xi, was a program for self-
cultivation that would allow each person to understand and access
the inherent goodness within that person. The diagram below sche-
matizes the two phases of the Eight-Step program. I constructed the
diagram to assist the reader in visualizing the connections within the
Eight-Step sequence; it does not exist in any Confucian writings.

Step One: Recognize (Investigate) Things and Affairs (Ge Wu), and Step Two: Extend One's Knowing (Zhi Zhi)

The first of the Eight Steps, as Zhu Xi conceived it, is to seek to understand broadly why both natural and moral principles work the way
they do. Scholars of the Learning of the Way felt there were insights
that could be discovered in the moral realm just as principles could ex-
plain why a blade of grass grows. The most perceptive classics on ethics can reveal such insights to the reader who is looking for them. The
Four Books were extracted by Zhu Xi to combine with the existing
canon of classics in order to facilitate greater access to humaneness,

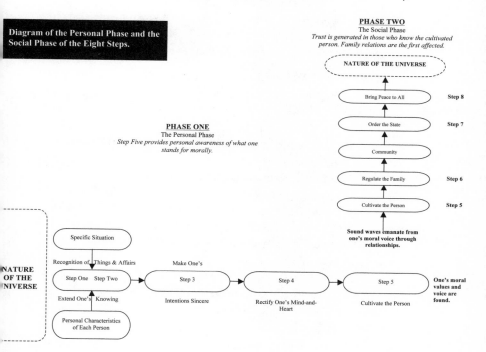

Diagram of the Personal Phase and the Social Phase of the Eight Steps.

PHASE TWO
The Social Phase
Trust is generated in those who know the cultivated person. Family relations are the first affected.

NATURE OF THE UNIVERSE

Bring Peace to All   Step 8

Order the State   Step 7

Community

Regulate the Family   Step 6

Cultivate the Person   Step 5

Sound waves emanate from one's moral voice through relationships.

PHASE ONE
The Personal Phase
Step Five provides personal awareness of what one stands for morally.

Specific Situation

Recognition of Things & Affairs   Make One's

NATURE OF THE UNIVERSE

Step One   Step Two   Step 3   Step 4   Step 5   **One's moral values and voice are found.**

Extend One's Knowing   Intentions Sincere   Rectify One's Mind-and-Heart   Cultivate the Person

Personal Characteristics of Each Person

rightness, ritual, and wisdom. These principles in one's subjective experience become manifest through human interaction.

The crucial first step is more an intellectual exercise than a spiritual practice. Cheng Yi's excerpts in *Reflections* note, "It is its [a clear mirror's] normal nature to reflect all things. . . . It is difficult not to have it reflect them. Similarly, the human mind-and-heart cannot but interact with the myriad things, and it is difficult not to have it engaged in thinking" (IV.48). Zhu Xi later elaborated on a similar point about principles.

In daily affairs, at all times and in all places, keep the mind-and-heart alert and do not let it wander. In this regard always observe principles, discuss what you seek and thoughtfully ponder it, deeply immerse yourself in it and go over and over it, and then you will be close to the teachings of sages and worthies. Gradually, you will gain a tacit understanding of them and naturally come to see that the characteristics with which we are endowed by the Dao of heaven are really within us. If you forsake what I call learning, then there will be nowhere else to apply your efforts.[3]

Studying human interaction or the natural world to access moral principles is a systematic intellectual exercise. As the *Reflections* anthology puts it, "books are intended to preserve and support one's mind-and-heart. . . . If one reads, his mind-and-heart will always maintain itself. If not, he will never understand moral principles" (III.74). Commentaries, in the Confucian tradition, were published as interlinear running interpretations of the meaning of each passage in a classic. The insights to be found in the passages of a classic and even in the commentaries of the accepted received editions of those classics were written by either sages or moral worthies, and their value to the reader lay in elucidating the moral principles that connected with the same qualities all humans possess innately.

Besides ethical classics, we can enter into careful discussions of historic events in order to determine the moral lessons that lie in the classics and the histories. As Zhu's *Conversations of Master Zhu, Arranged Topically* recorded the point, "Generally, in reading the Classics and histories, focus on the right and wrong. As you read the right, look for the wrong. As you read the wrong, look for the right. Afterward you'll understand moral principle."[4] In terms of learning from history, one should recall Hu Anguo's commentary from the Song period on the *Spring and Autumn Annals.* His interpretation that Confucius, when he wrote the *Annals,* was taking over the court's role in revising the state of Lu's records had been accepted by Zhu Xi, and when the Yuan dynasty established the standard for the Neo-Confucian curriculum, it included Hu's commentary that makes this point.

Students who took on the intellectual challenge of orally reciting classics from memory, Zhu felt, found that the deeper points in the text would then take on added meaning. The canon of recognized classics would likely need to be reread throughout one's life to plumb the variety of ethical principles that become visible as one ages and grows in personal experience. Extracting or recognizing moral principles from life and from the fund of past human experience in the classics and histories made it increasingly possible for people to live by moral action in their own lives.

Cheng Yi, Zhu's mentor, felt that there were three ways to recognize principles: (1) study books that elucidate moral principles; (2) discuss history so right and wrong actions, success and failure, can be determined; and (3) settle one's daily affairs in the proper way. Zhang Boxing (1652–1725), the great eighteenth-century Neo-Confucian scholar, added that the process began with the Four Books, then moved to the Five Classics, and turned later to the histories.

Zhu described the culmination of the first two steps in the Eight-Step program this way: "After exerting himself [in understanding physical and moral principle] for a long time, the individual will one day experience a breakthrough to integral comprehension. Then the qualities of all things, whether internal or external, refined or coarse, will be apprehended and the mind . . . will all be clearly manifested."[5] The beautiful sense of order and balance attained by the advanced learner is that an overall comprehension of principles in every part of one's life will transcend any distinction between knowledge of the inner self and the outer world. Zhu describes this in a special note to his commentary on the *Great Learning* by chapter and phrase. Each of us shall then see ourselves as part of nature and nature as similar to us. This occurs when one has been able to adequately (1) recognize (investigate) things and affairs, and (2) extend one's knowing.

Step two begins the internalization in one's mind of the physical and moral principles one has discovered from one's recognition of things and affairs. This stage of the journey still consists largely of intellectual growth and engagement with texts. Ethical classics assume a privileged place in a person's reading even compared to history, as they directly address moral principles.

How, then, does extending one's knowing fit into the process of self-cultivation? The attitude of reverence (*jing*) or inner seriousness is essential to guide this stage of one's joint intellectual and spiritual journey. The connection between extending knowledge and reverence, Zhu noted, is as necessary as two legs for walking.

> Abiding in reverence (*ju jing*) and exhaustive recognition of principles (*qiong li*) are the two phases of our moral self-cultivation, and these two phases should be mutually developed. Once there is the ability to exhaustively recognize principles, then persistent abiding [in reverence] will daily advance our moral self-cultivation; and

once we persist in abiding in this [reverence], then our moral self-cultivation will daily improve. It is just like a man with two legs: [when he walks] the left leg moves while the right leg is stationary, and when the right leg moves the left leg is stationary.[6]

In a sense, one is still a relative beginner at steps one and two, a toddler in the process of self-cultivation. One is still working to acquire the habit of continually extending knowledge while guided by a sense of direction from reverence. One without the other will not produce forward motion.

Step Three: Make One's Intentions Sincere

Neo-Confucians argued that disguising bad motives as good behavior is like trying to disguise a rotten egg; it is never effective for long. Despite this, we know that the temptation to tell a white lie about one's intentions — to oneself or to others — exists for anyone. No one sees a person's intention directly, which makes duplicity all the more alluring; eventually, however, one's intentions are revealed as clearly as smells and colors. Instead of waiting to be exposed, however, one could find guidance in the Neo-Confucian advice that, read literally, meant "even when alone, be watchful over yourself" (shen du) — a maxim repeated in Zengzi's commentary on the Great Learning and that appears again in the Mean. Less literally, however, Neo-Confucians saw this tenet as an honest monitoring of one's own unique development as one's humaneness is recovered from within.

Personal self-cultivation becomes the focus of more intensive work in the Eight-Step program beginning with step three, "Make Your Intentions Sincere." First and foremost it demands honesty from oneself about what one is doing, and why. This is not as simple as it may seem. Intentions are the predispositions, either consciously held or not, that precede any action, large or small. Thus step three, if applied to the present, for example, asks a person to critically examine his or her internal decisions even before taking action. Such honesty is what allows one to truly be oneself and to be genuine in relationships, as Zhu Xi noted: "Outwardly doing good things but inwardly in fact feeling quite different is 'self-deception.' It may be compared to a piece of copper that is coated with gold on the outside — inside it is not true gold."

Zhu continued elsewhere, "What about sincerity? It means to engage in neither self-deceit nor reckless abandon."[7]

The antidote to insincerity is the already identified part of self-cultivation that accompanies the recognition of principle, the attitude of mind called reverence, or being respectfully serious. A contemporary parallel in technology might be the instrument called the governor on a machine, which provides self-correcting feedback to an engine so that the movement can maintain itself at the proper speed or pressure. Applied to the work of self-cultivation, one's inner moral seriousness or reverence can likewise monitor the energy level of one's intention to detect any duplicity or self-deception and prevent it from compromising one's sincerity. As Cheng Yi is quoted in the *Reflections on Things at Hand* collection, "If one wants to avoid confusion and disturbance, one's mind must have a master. What can be its master? Reverence and reverence alone" (IV.48).

When a pupil of Cheng Hao (Cheng Yi's older brother) asked how to prevent personal worries from capturing his thoughts, his response clarified the role of a master within the mind.

> This is just like resisting robbers in a ruined house. Before you chase away the one who has entered from the east, another one comes from the west. They come in from all directions and there is no time to chase all of them away. The reason is that the house is exposed on all sides so that robbers can come in easily and there is no way for one to be the master of his own house and keep the situation under control.

He continued,

> It is like water coming into an empty vessel. Naturally, the water comes in. But if the vessel is filled with water, even if you put it under water, how can water get in? For whatever has a master inside is no longer empty. Since it is not empty, external troubles cannot come in. Then there will be nothing to worry you. (*Reflections* IV.10)

Zhu further commented on this idea: "If one's mind lacks a master, depravity from outside will come to fill it" (*Reflections* IV.48).

Reverence is the internal attitude of mind that one expresses outwardly as respect in relationships. It is the one ingredient required to begin and to maintain the sincerity of self-cultivation, and it needs to accompany all Eight Steps. Giving full attention to the moral problem at hand is the initial benefit of reverence, but it continues to assure that the serious concern expressed does indeed result in morally appropriate behavior.

Step Four: Rectify the Mind

All Confucians understood that living on a moral plane required the lifelong self-discipline to make conscious, thoughtful, and humane choices. Step four of the *Great Learning* outlines two basic methods of controlling the mind that composes one's self-discipline. Neither method creates value-free objectivity, but rather improves the empathic identification of principles in things and in oneself.

The first way to rectify the mind is to remain in conscious control of one's thoughts and willpower, which requires vigilant attention and practice in focusing and refocusing on the task at hand. The second is to prevent emotions from distorting one's thoughts and to curb the fleeting passions that, given free rein, could lead to biased and unbalanced judgment. The Chinese term for this combined "rectification" of mind is to "correct" — in the sense of making and keeping upright — just as the ninety-degree angles on its written character, *zheng* 正, illustrates.

If one wants to progress toward humaneness, one cannot afford to allow random, everyday thinking to lead even inadvertently to the inhumane treatment of others. As long as one's mind is consciously present, one has the ability to choose the respectful, empathetic alternative. Yet human beings are all too capable of reacting in relationships in so habitual a way as to give up the conscious operation of thought and willpower. Unfocused habit dulls awareness. When the mind is left to wander, although one might listen to someone, one really does not hear the other person at all. Zhu Xi was clear that any rote thinking in which unexamined habits dominate is not conscious, intentional thinking.

One Neo-Confucian, Zhang Zai, discussed preserving this moral consciousness by listening to the teacher within: "When one starts to rectify his mind, he should regard his own mind as a stern teacher.

Then he will be cautious in all his actions. If he can firmly hold on to this for a year or two, his mind [mind-and-heart] will naturally be rectified" (*Reflections* IV.67; the wording is Wing-tsit Chan's gendered translation). In other words, gradually internalizing a self-critical function for the improvement of your own mind can come about naturally if you keep your moral judgments conscious and unbiased for some time.

In Neo-Confucianism, human nature is seen in a positive light, and human minds are assumed to be capable of judging our own ideas without bias, but such clear judgment is hardest when one is highly emotional. Four emotions, in particular, must be monitored continuously for judgments to remain balanced and correct, and they are singled out in Zengzi's commentary attached to the *Great Learning*.

1. Anger
2. Fear
3. Fondness (doting, as directed at a daughter or son; Chinese term is *hao le*)
4. Worry

Everyone has had their ideas influenced by such feelings, and all are vulnerable to the distortions in judgment that can result. When any of these influences heavily cloud one's motivations, there is a need to regain composure before too much harm is done. Once balanced again, the mind is more able to judge clearly. As cited by Zhu in the *Further Reflections* collection of his sayings from the eighteenth century,

> Maintaining your self-cultivation for a long time will gradually lead to a congenial spirit; a congenial spirit will find one tender, generous, amiable, and agreeable. Anyone who hopes for this must eliminate his ill feelings and break up his anger, and be free of the adversity which invites opposition and attracts indignation. Personal and thorough recognition of things for a long time will gradually lead to the clarification of principle; perfect understanding will find one able to passively influence someone without openly criticizing them. Anyone who heeds this will be well-informed and influential, and free of the worry of rising up in contention and being rejected. Even more must we actively observe the principles

of things and deeply recognize our basic feelings; personally experience these things through your own faculties, carefully think about them through time — do these things and you will be free of the errors of bias and deceit.[8]

Resolve and Reflection

Disciplined motivation is critical in the first four steps of the Eight-Step self-cultivation program. In Confucian literature more broadly, the subject of "resolution to act" (lit., establishing one's resolve, or *li zhi*) in fact became a leitmotif. There was no Sabbath in Confucianism set aside as a weekly reminder to live up to one's moral ideals; instead, devotion to one's family, the right choice of friends, and, most of all, one's sense of full responsibility for one's own conduct and character were a person's most obvious moral touchstones. Teachers and mentors were available in most communities, and many in fact compiled their own books of favorite quotations for the edification of present and future students. One example from the nineteenth century will illustrate: while he ran the Dragon Gate Academy in Shanghai from 1866 to 1880, headmaster Liu Xizai (1813–1881) compiled a collection of sayings to guide his students, titled *Lessons on Maintaining Resolve*. It began with the argument that "the permanence of willpower comes from exercising it," to inform and exhort students that like a muscle, willpower strengthens through repeated use. Books filled with selected Confucian sayings and quotations like this one became a lasting legacy of hundreds of fine teachers, and they frequently highlighted personal resolve. Maintaining one's resolve throughout the difficulties of practice allows a person to work on the first five steps consistently, and hence to slowly but steadily nurture the process of becoming humane.

Yet the kind of balanced judgment called for in rectifying the mind requires more than a strong, persevering will; the ability to reflect is equally important. The second paragraph of the *Great Learning* indicates that reflection in turn presumes a state of mind called being at peace. The peace of mind advocated in the *Great Learning* is itself a kind of composure. Such calm preparedness is akin to the attitude of those who are "unflappable" in a crisis — they maintain mental composure in the midst of tense action. Similarly, a sage would be composed in his or her activity.

The important role of imagination in Confucian ethics begins with empathy, which requires a person to imagine how one would feel if in the same situation described by another. The metaphorical possibilities that are liberated by imagination transport thinking to the invisible moral or spiritual plane. One perceptive Neo-Confucian, Ye Cai (fl. 1248 CE), chose the physical image of a serene pond to help imagine the purpose of reflection in the *Great Learning*. He asked the reader to think of the physical properties of water, and when it can and cannot reflect. "Brilliance and intelligence result if the mind is tranquil and calm. Still water can reflect. But running water cannot. The principle is the same" (*Reflections* IV.69).

One can apply this imaginative insight to relationships. For example, suppose a friend or loved one is trying to communicate a complex need or desire to you. If your own desires, your own ego, and your own needs fill your mind while you attempt to listen, you are not likely to hear an unfiltered version of what that person is saying. But if you are as serene as a quiet pond, you are more likely to reflect, mirror-like, the reality opposite you. Eliminating the disruption of your own interests allows a serene mind to more sincerely and correctly perceive what is communicated, which thus makes it much easier to humanely put oneself in the shoes of another.

Step Five: Cultivating the Person

The fifth step mandates a regular practice of *sustaining* our honest intentions and correct actions. In the first four steps one has established a practice of recognizing, extending, making sincere, and rectifying. The next step, cultivating the person, includes control of the body (note that the term for body in step five, *shen*身, also means "person" or "being"). Zhu Xi viewed anger or rage as something that would unbalance the mind-and-heart. Step five maintains the role of one's innate luminous virtue in the face of desires and emotions that could otherwise obscure one's inner goodness. Resolutely maintaining the values that one has made upright in step four means that one has found one's moral values and voice and will thereafter know what one stands for in the complex and unpredictable world of social relationships.

Many people do good deeds and are generally honest in their relationships, yet they do not achieve the consistency of moral action that would distinguish a truly humane person. The difference is like that between a professional athlete and a "weekend warrior"; consistency comes with professional training. As Zhu put it, "There are those who only know to make their intentions sincere but are unable to keep close watch over the preservation of their minds: and so they are incapable of *maintaining* their inner correctness and of cultivating their persons."[9]

The analogy of the serious athlete versus the casual one shows that semi-conscious habitual actions, or going through the motions, are not enough. In fact, passive, habitual moral action is precisely what step five eliminates. The traditional commentary attributed to Zengzi points out that "if the mind is not present one looks but does not see, listens but does not hear, eats but does not appreciate the flavor."[10] Presence of mind, or fully paying attention, is an attitude with which one should approach others. Like a highly focused participant in a game of chess, this attitude serves as an "inner mental attentiveness" to maintain conscious control over intentionality and moral action.

Confucius made clear that truly humane conduct requires moral responsibilities, but such responsibilities are not a pro-forma observation of a list of rules and prohibitions. As he put it, "Becoming [morally] authoritative is self-originating — how could it originate in others?" (*Analects* 12.1). That is, rather than submitting to an imposed external authority, this growth must come from inside. Neo-Confucians after 1000 CE were especially insistent that right thinking is inseparable from willpower, motivation, and feelings. Confucians considered the behavioral change present in practicing a virtue to actually be part of understanding it. In his *Reflections on Things at Hand*, Zhu selected a passage from Zhang Zai arguing that anyone attaining "humaneness in the highest degree" would become a living exemplar of the behavioral norms of humaneness and would be described as "respectful, reverent, inclined to restraint, and yielding" (XI.18). In other words, ethical understanding is both internal and visibly tied to one's conduct.

Confucius himself gave some guidance for the sort of self-discipline that would prevent one from doing wrong each day. Asked for details on what would be necessary to practice humaneness, Confucius answered, in *Analects* 12.1, "Do not look at anything that violates ritual propriety; do not listen to anything that violates ritual propriety; do not speak about anything that violates ritual propriety; do not do anything that violates ritual propriety." Fifteen hundred years later Cheng Yi transformed this advice into a list of admonitions that he could review regularly for his own edification. The term "propriety" in his passage below refers to the ethical norms of society one has chosen to live by.

Admonition on Seeing:
The mind is originally vacuous [that is, in a state of
     consciousness]
It responds to things without leaving any observable trace.
There are essentials in controlling it [the mind],
The foremost of which is the regulation of its seeing.
If obscurations of selfish desires multiply before one's eyes,
One's mind will be lured away.
Control its external activities
So its internal state will be secured.
Discipline yourself and return to propriety
After a long time, you will be sincere.

Admonition on Hearing:
If one is tempted by the knowledge of external things and is
     overcome by material desires,
He will lose the good nature he has received.
Eminent are those who are the first to understand.
They know on what to rest and are calm.
Guard against depravity and preserve sincerity.
Do not listen to what is contrary to propriety.

Admonition on Speech:
The activities of the human mind
Are expressed through words.
If in one's expression he allows no rashness or falsehood,
He will be tranquil and concentrated within.
More especially, words are a turning point
That can lead to hostility or amity.
Good and evil fortune, and glory and shame,
Are all invited by them.
When they are defective by being lighthearted,
          they will be heedless.
And when they are defective by being too many,
          they will be fragmentary.

To lose control of oneself is to violate the principle of things.
What one does to others will be done to him.
Do not say anything contrary to propriety.
Respectfully obey the injunction of the Sage.

Admonition on Action:
Wise men know the subtle, incipient, activating force of things,
And therefore are sincere in their thoughts.
Resolute scholars exert themselves in their actions
And hold fast to [their minds-and-hearts] in whatever they do.
He who follows principles will enjoy peace and abundance.
He who follows desires will be in danger.
Do not forget this for a moment.
Conduct yourself with apprehension and caution.
If one's cultivation matches one's originally good nature,
In the end he will be the same as the sages and worthies.
  (*Reflections* V.3)

The Cult of the Accomplished Student

The *Analects* was the oldest of the Four Books, and one important reason it never became outmoded in Confucian education was because the lives of Confucius' immediate disciples as portrayed there provided concrete guidance for the difficult process of self-cultivation. This was particularly true in the case of Confucius' favorite student, Hui, who remained a kind of case study in how to conduct step five of the Eight Steps and in what it means to cultivate the person.

Neo-Confucians, in fact, built a small cult around the personality of this exemplar of successful self-cultivation. Cheng Hao, in particular, warned students that leaping ahead of the *Analects* to the *Mencius,* the third of the Four Books, was a mistake, albeit a tempting one. To improve the students on their way to sagehood, Cheng advised them to turn, instead, to the specific examples recorded in the *Analects* of decisions made by Hui. His experiences were clearly recorded and available to guide a student to live morally, which required undergoing a difficult process of discovery and recognition of moral principles.

One can find within the *Analects* a few traits about Hui: first, he did not transfer his anger to others (6.3), and second, he did not repeat a mistake (6.3). Thus when Hui did become angry, he never allowed his feelings to resurface in an unrelated interaction with someone else—for example, at home or in the marketplace. Such an action sounds simple enough: leave family issues at home and do not bring work issues to the home. And yet how many people bring their work stress to their interactions after work? How many dysfunctional personal relationships overflow into professional problems? This type of self-control should apply to any of the most common seven feelings distinguished by Neo-Confucians: pleasure, anger, sorrow, joy, love, hate, and desire. The Song-era Neo-Confucians excerpted in *Reflections on Things at Hand* were careful to describe what it was like to work diligently on humaneness yet remain short of sagehood, and Hui became the test case: "The sage 'apprehends without thinking and hits upon what is right without effort.' Hui had to think before apprehending, and had to make an effort before hitting upon what is right. The difference between him and the sage is as little as a moment of breathing. What was lacking in him was that he held on to [goodness] but was not yet completely transformed [into goodness itself]. Since he loved to learn, had he lived longer, he would have achieved transformation in a short time" (II.3). Admiration for such an exemplary student clearly facilitated the efforts of new students working to cultivate the person. Ironically, Hui's shortcomings made him a more effective example; he was still a work in progress. He was a man who still had to *decide* not to transfer his anger and not to repeat a mistake. A sage, on the other hand, would not need to think about it and choose among alternatives at all—the sage would automatically do the right thing.

Another example of Hui's accomplishments that help students self-cultivate is a passage in the *Analects* where Hui tells Confucius what he would most like to do in life—namely, to be able to refrain from bragging about his abilities or exaggerating his accomplishments. Unlike a sage—and like the rest of us—Hui still had to consciously work to overcome these temptations, and that is why it is helpful to study his life. As Cheng Yi states in *Reflections on Things at Hand,* "Since he was unable to 'hit upon what is right without effort,' or to 'give his mind-and-heart free rein without overstepping the [moral] boundaries,' this means he made mistakes. But he was intelligent and strong. Therefore, whenever he did anything wrong, he never failed to correct it right away. Thus he never reached the point requiring repentance. . . . The way of learning is none other than to change one's ways immediately and follow the good as soon as one realizes that one has done something wrong" (V.4).

The Host-Guest Metaphor

Confucius praised the accomplishments of Hui in the following way: "The Master said, 'As for Hui, he could go three months without in his mind ever departing from humaneness. The others can do so for a day or a month, but that is all!'" (Watson, *Analects* 6.7). Zhang Zai's excerpt in the *Reflections on Things at Hand* anthology rephrased this fifteen hundred years later and added a metaphor noting that having nothing in one's heart contrary to humaneness for three months was comparable to making humaneness the host, while shorter visits by humaneness in their hearts made it like a guest. Zhu Xi, in his own later commentary on Zhang's metaphor, continued, "Not to have anything contrary to humaneness means that humaneness is inside the person and is the host or master. But it is not entirely at home and sometimes leaves him. To achieve humaneness for a day or a month means that humaneness is outside of the person and is a guest. Although it sometimes comes in, it does not stay long" (IV.64). The host is also the master of the house (and in fact the Chinese term *zhu* 主 meant both "master" and "host," depending upon the context in which it was used, so the two meanings easily conflate as the reader sees that the host welcoming guests to a home can also be considered the master of the house). This accomplishment of maintaining nothing but humaneness in one's heart for three months remained the gold standard for later Confucians working on their own self-cultivation.

Unlike these passages about Hui in the *Analects*, the *Mencius* does not address specific details of how someone like Hui practiced his love of learning. The Neo-Confucians created a blueprint of the Eight Steps mentioned in the *Great Learning*, then instructed students to read the *Analects* for real-life stories of the experiences of Confucius' disciples. As one commentator selected in the *Reflections on Things at Hand* anthology concluded around 1250 CE, "What is beyond the ability to have for three months nothing contrary to humaneness [in one's heart] is a quality belonging to one who is great and completely transformed so that he *is humaneness itself*" (IV.64; emphasis added). This is the ultimate stage of cultivating the person and can be considered coterminous with sagehood.

Another of Hui's statements preserved in the *Analects* was understood by many Neo-Confucians to mean that Hui, despite his unerring dedication, did not attain humaneness in his short life (he died at the age of thirty-two).

> Yan Hui, with a deep sigh, said, "The more I look up at it, the higher it soars; the more I penetrate into it, the harder it becomes. I am looking at it in front of me, and suddenly it is behind me. The Master is good at drawing me forward a step at a time; he broadens me with culture and disciplines my behavior through the observance of ritual propriety. Even if I wanted to quit, I could not. And when I have exhausted my abilities, it is as though something rises up right in front of me, and even though I want to follow it, there is no road to take. (9.11)

The "it" Hui was searching for was the attainment of humaneness, which, if sustained over time, constituted sagehood. One great strength of the Neo-Confucians during the Song dynasty was their refinement of the practical process of how to conduct the program of self-cultivation. Among other nuances, they were able to distinguish different levels of achievement among the disciples of Confucius, based on each student's questions and answers to the Master as described in the *Analects*.

Sequence Is Appropriate to Refined Levels of Self-Cultivation

To some extent, the subtle meaning of what lies ahead in building humaneness can be grasped only by the advanced practitioner who has become adept at self-cultivation. Short of this high level of achievement, perhaps only the metaphorical imagination has the capacity to provide a glimpse of becoming one with humaneness. The traditionally accepted commentator on the *Great Learning,* whom Zhu Xi was convinced was Zengzi, elaborated, citing a poem that appears in the *Classic of Odes* that suggests the systematic work required of cultivating oneself was practiced among the ancient sage kings and princes.

> There is our elegant and accomplished prince —
> As if cutting and filing,
> As if chiseling and polishing,
> [So he cultivates himself!]

Zengzi continued, " 'As if cutting and filing' [the bone] speaks to the process of learning; 'as if chiseling and polishing' [the jade] to the process of self-cultivation."[11]

Years later Zhu added his own analysis to Zengzi's and highlighted an insight in the *Great Learning*—namely that the *proper sequence* in studying or cultivating oneself is one critical dimension in making this process succeed. Expanding on the gemology metaphor, Zhu emphasized the proper order of events by showing how to transform a rough gem into a jewel: "One cuts with a knife or a saw and chisels with a mallet or chisel to pare an object to a desired shape. One files with a rasp or a plane and polishes with sand or stone to give an object a smooth finish. In crafting bone and horn, one cuts then files repeatedly. In crafting jade and stone, one chisels then polishes repeatedly. Both of these cases show that in crafting an object there is a proper sequence according to which the object is brought to perfection."[12]

Each person can aspire to the ideal of the utmost good that is possible in the cultivation of a sage, but rubbing a rough piece of jade with another stone of identical hardness will yield no increase in luster. Cultivation of the person requires enough prior learning to acquire a knowledge of people, and it entails a strictly ordered, sequential process of refinement. The only quotation from the Neo-Confucian Shao Yong in the *Reflections on Things at Hand* anthology speaks to this issue by elaborating on a line from the *Classic of Odes* (line 184), "There are other hills whose stones are good for grinding tools; there are other hills whose stones are good for working jade."

> In explaining the saying, "Stones in the yonder hills can polish jade," Yaofu [Shao Yong] said, "Jade is a gentle and smooth thing. If two pieces of jade are used to polish each other, neither will be polished. It is necessary to get a hard and rough thing to polish them. Take the case of a [morally] superior man associating with an inferior man. As the inferior man encroaches upon him, he will cultivate and examine himself, become cautious toward the inferior man and avoid him, stimulate his own mind and harden his nature, improve himself in order to prevent any future trouble. Then the principle of the saying will become clear." (*Reflections* V.15)

The experienced teacher will push the student with increasingly challenging work, but only at a pace such that the student is able to assimilate points. Sima Guang, in the early Song period, wrote the first commentary on the *Great Learning,* and Cheng Hao singled out the *Great Learning* partly because he saw that sequential stages were distinguished in its progression. Cheng Yi put Cheng Hao's affinity for the short *Great Learning* classic this way:

> There were many students in the Master's [Cheng Hao's] school. The Master's words were simple, easy, and easily understood. Both the morally accomplished worthy and the student benefited from them, as if all drank from the river, each to the limit of his capacity. In teaching people, from the extension of knowledge to knowing where to abide, from the sincerity of intentions to bringing peace to all, and from sprinkling and sweeping the floor and answering questions to investigating principle to the utmost and fully developing one's nature, the Master followed a definite order, for he was afraid that students of the day would neglect what is near at hand and run after the remote, peep at what is lofty while they were on the low level, and consequently would easily regard themselves as superior, and in the end fail to accomplish anything. (*Reflections* XIV.17)

The correct order of learning texts, and the correct pace of mastering them, instills self-restraint in the learner that leads to gradual improvement.

Extension on the Basis of Similarity in Kind

Imagination is another essential element of cultivating the person to extend one's humaneness. There are specific attitudes that can block one's imagination from seeing the similarity between ideas that should otherwise allow one to progress. The similarity between the mind-and-heart of a sage such as Confucius, for example, and the nature of Heaven and Earth would be one such parallel a person should be able to apprehend. Cheng Hao singled out four kinds of attitudes that are obstacles in the search for sagehood: arbitrary or capricious thinking, as it leaves an opening in one's thinking for selfish ideas and therefore must be eliminated; egotistical and authoritarian thinking are two more, which also invite the unwanted impositions of one's own views on otherwise balanced judgments; and obstinate or stubborn thinking, which binds the mind-and-heart to the confines of fixed attitudes and prejudices.

An affectionate attitude toward one's parents can provide a natural basis for each person to extend that affectionate feeling to humaneness to all older people, and even to all human beings. The reason, Neo-Confucians argued, was that the class of "people in general" is similar enough to parents that each person can generalize one's parental affection to others who are not one's parents. Love for parents teaches love for humanity. The next step above being humane to all people was considered close enough to "love for all living things" that it was natural for Confucians committed to self-cultivation to then develop a love for all creatures. As Cheng Hao is quoted in *Reflections on Things at Hand*, "The man of humaneness regards Heaven and Earth and all creatures as one body. To him there is nothing that is not himself. . . . Therefore to be charitable and to assist all things is the function of a sage" (I.20). One can imagine an expanding set of concentric circles reaching farther and farther from the self, eventually embracing all of nature.

Progress in increasing one's humaneness would then lead to emotional, moral, and spiritual transformation. As the *Mencius* pointed out, "People all have things that they will not bear. To extend this reaction to that which they will bear is humaneness" (7B31). The closer a person comes to becoming one with humaneness, the more humaneness is not just mentally understood, but also becomes part of one's identity. It cannot be accomplished all at once. When that love has been practiced and extended so that one is capable of generalizing it to humane love for all living things in the universe, one begins to approach sagehood.

Zhang Zai wrote an advanced Neo-Confucian essay on the substance of humaneness in which he argued that once one begins to identify with humaneness, the process can be nourished by continuing to understand the moral principles in passages of the ethical classics. This insightful document, "The Western Inscription," was originally titled "Correcting Obstinacy," and in it Zhang reveals where this advanced work eventually leads.

The Western Inscription

Heaven is my father and Earth is my mother, and even such a small creature as I finds an intimate place in their midst.

Therefore that which extends throughout the universe I regard as my body, and that which directs the universe I consider as my nature.

All people are my brothers and sisters, and all things are my companions.

The great ruler [the emperor] is the eldest son of my parents [Heaven and Earth], and the great ministers are his stewards. Respect the aged — this is the way to treat them as elders should be treated. Show affection toward the orphaned and the weak — this is the way to treat them as the young should be treated. The sage identifies his virtue with that of Heaven and Earth, and the worthy is the best [among the children of Heaven and Earth]. Even those who are tired and infirm, crippled or sick, those who have no brothers or children, wives or husbands, are all my brothers who are in distress and have no one to turn to.

When the time comes, to keep himself from harm — this is the care of a son. To rejoice in Heaven and have no anxiety — this is filiality at its purest.

One who disobeys [the principle of Heaven] violates virtue. One who destroys is a robber. One who promotes evil lacks [moral] capacity. But one who puts his moral nature into practice and brings his physical existence to complete fulfillment can match [Heaven and Earth].

One who knows the principles of transformation will skillfully carry forward the undertakings [of Heaven and Earth], and one who penetrates spirit to the highest degree will skillfully carry out their will.

Do nothing shameful even in the recesses of your own home and thus bring dishonor to it. Preserve the mind and nourish the nature and thus [serve them] with untiring effort.

The great Yu shunned pleasant wine but attended to the protection and support of his parents. Border Warden Ying cared for the young and thus extended his love to his own kind.

Emperor Shun's merit lay in delighting his parents with unceasing effort, and Shensheng's reverence [Shensheng was a prince who committed suicide when falsely accused of murdering his father] was demonstrated when he awaited punishment without making an attempt to escape.

Zeng Can received his body from his parents and reverently kept it intact throughout life, while [Yin] Boqi vigorously obeyed his father's command.

Wealth, honor, blessing, and benefit are meant for the enrichment of my life, while poverty, humble station, care, and sorrow will be my helpmates to fulfillment.

In life I follow and serve [Heaven and Earth]. In death I will be at peace.[13]

Neo-Confucian teachers such as Cheng Hao said that when they heard the bray of a donkey or the whinny of a horse, they felt commonality with those animals. Zhou Dunyi, feeling kinship with the plant world, even refused to cut the grass outside his window. Of course, this humane empathy for nature based on the extension of one's inner humaneness will initially seem unreachable or even absurd. One begins self-cultivation with simply trying to simultaneously recognize principles in nature and in oneself. Even talented and serious new students of Confucianism were often kept from studying such ecstatic statements as the "The Western Inscription" for some time. Access to the *Great Learning,* with its systematic Eight-Step program of ordered instructions, might also be withheld for half a year or more in favor of the primers that served as preparatory ladders to the Four Books. One should first study more basic texts such as the *Mencius,* and passages in it such as the following that address an idea developed in more advanced texts: "Mencius said, 'That by which humans differ from animals is slight. The masses abandon it. The exemplary person prefers it. . . . He [the sage] *acted out of* humaneness and rightness; he *did not act out* humaneness and rightness" (4B19; emphasis added). Zhu Xi felt that correct learning allowed a morally clarified person to act from the source of these two innate moral principles, humaneness and rightness, as if they were second nature to that person.

CHAPTER 4

The Three Steps of Social Development

The complete text of the *Great Learning* has the following paragraph at its conclusion: "From the Son of Heaven [the emperor] down to the common people, they all as one take cultivating the person to be the root. How could it be that the root be disturbed and yet have the branch remain undisturbed? Never should the important be treated as trivial; never should the trivial be treated as important." Zhu Xi explained that the word "important" in this final sentence should refer to the "family." The preceding cultivation of the person was then linked directly to the social identity and influence of a given person in the family and tied to the health of the family. Because all people in the Confucian state should practice the first five steps of personal cultivation, and because their luminous virtue would then be visible in their lives, everyone would treat his kinsmen as kinsmen, everyone would treat his elders as elders — so that throughout the empire all would be tranquil.

Step Six: Regulate the Family

The advanced kind of empathy called "similarity in kind" is precisely the basis on which cultivation of self can also become regulation of the family. Zhu argued that the love of a parent could be extended to all people, and he illustrated the point using the sixth of the Eight Steps: "When he understands how to be humane to people, he will extend this feeling, on the basis of similarity in kind, to loving all things, for being humane to all people and loving all things are similar in kind. . . . For example, cultivation of the person will extend to regulation of the family; regulation of the family will extend to ordering the state. It is just one completed step, then another step."[1] Clearly Zhu's notion of regulating the family is something other than ruling with an iron fist. What is the connection between "regulating" and "loving"?

Confucius himself was once asked rather insistently to define how an exemplary person (*junzi*) would cultivate himself.

> "He cultivated himself so as to become fully attentive," was his answer.
>
> But the student continued: "This and nothing more?"
>
> Confucius then added, "He cultivates himself so as to ease the lot of others."
>
> "This and nothing more?" was the student's response a second time.
>
> Finally Confucius ventured, "He cultivates himself so as to ease the lot of all people. Even [the legendary] Yao and Shun would have found this difficult." (*Analects* 14.42)

For Confucius the notion of a morally exemplary person presumed a laudable level of self-cultivation, and the extension of one's inherently relational self was natural as self-cultivation developed.

It is from one's affection for one's parents that self-cultivation initially extends one's love and respect to older siblings and to all other family members. Because these family connections are reciprocal, respect for others builds one's self-respect. Neo-Confucian educators insisted that the interrelationship between parent and child should be consciously acknowledged as the source of mutual respect in all relationships. Citing the *Record of Rites* as excerpted in his *Elementary Learning,* Zhu made the following point: "There is nothing the exemplary person does not reverence. And reverence for the self or person is the greatest of all. He is in his person a branch of his parents — can any son not have this self-respect? If he is not able to respect his own person he is wounding his parents."[2] The carefully calibrated terms of address in Chinese society for designating the variety of uncles and aunts, cousins, nephews, nieces, and other descendents — all terms of respect that are stronger the closer the blood distance from oneself — naturally socialized a young person into the graded levels of loving respect that orders or regulates family relationships.

In his *Elementary Learning* manual Zhu also chose a poignant quotation from the Han dynasty *Classic of Family Reverence* when discussing parents: "Parents gave one life; no bond could be stronger. They watch over their child with utmost care; no love could be greater.

Therefore to love others without first loving one's parents is to act against virtue. To reverence other men without first reverencing one's parents is to act against propriety."[3] In addition, Zhu recommended to students certain sections of *The Classic of Odes* as a valuable resource in beginning self-cultivation, because those sections dealt with matters of personal cultivation and regulation of the family.

Mencius understood what evolutionary biology now confirms — that humans are born with the predisposition to acts of reciprocal altruism among kin. The Neo-Confucians accepted the family as the structural core of social organization, and their rituals reinforce kinship categories. More supernatural beliefs remained diffused, with no independent personnel and organization of their own, but they served to add awesome power to the secular social institutions into which they were diffused. Ancestor worship, for example, accompanied filial piety, and the souls of departed ancestors were allowed to play a role in the perpetuation of the family. The social networks like the community compacts promoted by Neo-Confucians were understood to be based upon the family and to provide services and protection in local society below the perimeter of state power.

Zhou Dunyi, one of the Five Masters of the Northern Song and Zhu Xi's Neo-Confucian predecessor, argued that creating harmony in an extended family was actually more difficult than governing any political entity. Still, Zhou stated, it is crucial to see that one is an extension of the other: "In order to see how a ruler governs his empire, we observe the government of his family. In order to see how he governs his family, we observe how he governs himself. To be correct in one's person means to be sincere in one's heart" (*Reflections* VIII.1). The logic is a chain analogy or a sorites: the heart is to the person as the person is to the family as the family is to the empire. Song-period Neo-Confucians anticipated that the model provided by rulers would be emulated by the ruled. This is the logic of the *Great Learning* text.

In general, the elders in traditional China were entrusted with the responsibility to oversee communal ceremonies that preserved common social norms. Young people were exposed to teachers and other mentors outside the family who confirmed the worthwhile values taught at home. Elders oversaw life-cycle rituals that would inform the unavoidable transitions along the way from youth to old age. Ideally, elders, as preservers of tradition, were both personal models and repositories of wisdom regarding what acting humanely with consistency would be like.

In the Song period, girls commonly underwent a coming-of-age initiation called pinning, when they were engaged to marry. This ceremony commonly occurred by age fifteen, although boys came of age in a capping ceremony somewhere between ages fifteen and twenty. Zhu outlined a model of both ceremonies in his manual, *Family Rituals*.

In the girl's case, at dawn on the day of the pinning ceremony the young girl combed her hair into a topknot, then called on her elders. Many relatives and elders assembled, and the mother of the girl acted as the presiding female for the pinning ceremony. Some three days before the ceremony, the mother had selected a female relative who was considered wise and decorous to serve as a sponsor for the pinning of the girl. The initiate put her hair in two topknots for the ceremony itself and wore a gown, then stood facing south in a room off the main hall. When the sponsor arrived, the mother invited her to enter the hall where the ceremony took place. As a sign of her formal initiation into adulthood, the sponsor would beckon to the initiate to go to a mat on the floor, then placed a cap on the initiate's head and inserted a pin in her hair. The initiate then went back to the side room to don a jacket that had been prepared by the family. At that point the girl was told ceremonially some variation of the following by the sponsor: "On an excellent day of an auspicious month, you wear head gear for the first time. Set aside your childish ideas and comply with the virtues of womanhood. Then your years will be blessed, and your fortune will be great." The initiate then offered wine in ritual sacrifice, at which point the sponsor formally gave the initiate her adult name. After the naming ceremony the sponsor was entertained as an honored guest of the girl's family.

For a young man's initiation into adulthood, as Zhu recommended it, a presiding man who was probably the head of the family reported the event to an offering hall three days before the ceremony and then personally invited a prominent male friend well versed in ritual to be the sponsor at the ritual. The sponsor then ceremonially recited the same words used in a girl's pinning ceremony to the male initiate regarding the setting aside of childish ideas and complying, in the boy's case, with the virtues of manhood. But new garments, beginning with a cap, were put on in three ceremonial kneelings that concluded with the young man donning either an official's or a scholar's robes. The sponsor continued,

> **Sponsor [praying]:** The fine wine is pure. The excellent offerings have superior flavors. Receive them with a bow and offer them in sacrifice to affirm your good fortune. May you receive Heaven's blessings and longevity.
> [The initiate bows twice and receives a bow in response from the sponsor. The young man then kneels. He offers wine in sacrifice, stands, and kneels in the opposite direction. He bows twice facing south, and the sponsor bows in reply. Finally, a bow from the initiate to an assistant in the ceremony is answered by a bow from the assistant.]
>
> **Sponsor:** The ceremony is now completed. On this auspicious day of this excellent month, I pronounce your adult name (*zi*). May this name be greatly honored, may you be a gentleman and gain eminence, act correctly, and achieve greatness. Preserve forever what you are receiving.
> [The sponsor then calls him by the term of address indicating his sibling order in his family.]
>
> **Initiate:** Although I, [so-and-so], am not quick, I dare but reverently obey your instructions morning and evening.[4]

Following the ceremony, the newly initiated man went out in public to be presented to his father's friends and local elders.

Such rituals for both young men and women were reciprocal in the sense that the older generation acknowledged that the young initiates would thereafter be treated as adults and assume adult responsibilities. For the initiated, their adult status meant that they would observe the basic Confucian loyalties and reverence in relationships: the filial duties of a son or daughter, the authority of his or her older siblings, his or her loyalty as a subject under the ruling officials, and his or her recognition of the veneration required of all persons of the older generation. These were foundational Confucian virtues, and each initiate acknowledged them as he or she entered adult society through the capping or pinning ceremonies.

Step Seven: Order the State

Classical Confucian texts addressed how the extended family could become a natural basis for social and political order. The *Mean* stated,

> If one cultivates one's person, the Way will be established there-from; if one esteems those of superior character, there will be no confusion; if one treats one's kin as kin, one's many uncles and brothers will harbor no ill will; if one respects the high ministers, there will be no deception; if one is inclusive of the whole assembly of ministers, the scholar-officials will repay one's courtesies two-fold; if one treats the common people as one's children, the various clans will be much encouraged; if one attracts the various artisans, [the] materials and the skills needed to use them will be sufficient; if one is tolerant of those from afar, people from distant quarters will flock to one; if one cherishes the various nobles, the world will hold one in awe. (Chapter 20)

Although it was common to accept these values in principle, Neo-Confucians complained that society's leaders did not implement these ideas in practice. The impediment to implementation often originated with corrupt power brokers at the village level. The equity of taxation, for example, was frequently compromised by landlords who falsified the correct registration of the boundaries of their fields. Officials at the provincial or prefectural level had to be ever vigilant to prevent malfeasance. Zhu Xi had firsthand experience as a local official and attributed public misconduct to personal failings: "The reason why the world's affairs are never completed is simply because we suffer from being lazy and selfish. Consider [the ancient practice of] mark-ing boundaries." Zhu knew that classical Confucians such as Mencius had already addressed this critical point about the equity of land taxa-tion when the latter gave advice to a duke: "Now benevolent govern-ment must begin with setting field boundaries. If the field boundaries are not straightly set, the well fields will not be equal, and the grain income will not be even. For this reason cruel rulers and corrupt of-ficials are necessarily lax about setting the field boundaries" (*Mencius* III.A.3). Zhu continued, "If it is not done, how can we be completely free of corruption. Still, if there are ten parts corruption we must get rid of nine parts. . . . But today people would rather suffer the ten parts of corruption. . . . . Clearly [we live in] this world, and [in] this country, yet no one is willing to look on it as they do their own family."[5]

The Neo-Confucian idea of a compact made by several families to create a community organization on a scale about the size of a hamlet or a small clan village was one innovation in the traditional social structure designed to meet the difficulties in extending moral conduct beyond the family. Such a community organization would be independent of the official power of the state and could establish a mutual agreement to promote an ordered ritual framework beyond each family's internal kinship organization. Zhu drew from existing precedents of extended-family compacts to create a model that was voluntary and appealed to the families' self-interests, largely because it added security and diminished some causes of social and economic strife.

The major characteristic of the community compact Zhu promoted was a ritual communal practice joined to an ethical code. Ritual took the form of a monthly meal together, including enjoyable activities after the meal; the code of ethics consisted of four general injunctions that all members were to follow. The first injunction was to admonish each other to behave virtuously — including not evading taxes; the second was to correct each other's (unspecified) wrongs; the third was to agree to be reverent and follow established customs in public interactions with one another; and finally, the families were to assist one another in times of illness or crisis. In addition, Zhu's original draft of the Community Compact also singled out six precepts for moral behavior that were more specific. Variations of this agreement appear in the Ming (1368–1644) and Qing dynasties that followed.

During the early fourteenth century, for example, the Ming dynasty's peasant-monk founder and first emperor, Ming Taizu, added an idea to the formulation of compacts that allowed the transmission of the essential principles of Zhu's community covenant, including the six initial precepts, to the nonliterate majority. The privileges of membership would then be open to a more inclusive and egalitarian population than just the intelligentsia. The first emperor of the Ming promoted the following.

In each village and *li* [local grouping of families] a bell with a wooden clapper shall be prepared. Old persons, disabled persons unable to function normally, or blind persons shall be selected and guided by children to walk through the *li* holding the bell. If there are no such persons in the *li,* then they shall be selected from other *li.* Let them shout loudly so that everyone can hear, urging people to do good and not violate the law. Their message is: "Be filial to your parents, respect elders and superiors, live in harmony with neighbors, instruct and discipline children and grandchildren, be content with your occupation, commit no wrongful acts."[6]

That last sentence lists the Six Precepts from Zhu Xi's original Community Compact. Socially motivated Neo-Confucians such as Wang Yangming and his reform-minded followers during and following the Ming period continued to foster community compacts as one aspect of the transition between step six of the Eight Steps, regulating the family, and step seven, the order of the state, as outlined in the *Great Learning.*

However, a broad adoption of the compact model did not take effect as hoped. The increasingly despotic power of the Ming and then Qing emperorships forced the community compacts slowly into the service of state power. By the Qing takeover in the 1600s, the compact had been co-opted into formal public meetings that addressed only the standards of harmonious social interaction that the ruling Manchu conquerors expected from a docile populace. Local notables spoke in villages on the first and fifteenth of each month, publicly stating ten new precepts added to Zhu Xi's original six, as a reminder to the people that the state demanded their obedience. This sixteen-provision Sacred Edict of the Emperor of the Qing instructed citizens to be moral, frugal, and diligent, to resolve their differences in a civil way without litigation, and to cooperate for mutual protection. Such a self-serving and didactic series of lectures was a far cry from the voluntaristic community organizations that Zhu had promoted, which were antithetical to indoctrination. Transformed from its original structure into a means of institutional enforcement of government rules, these lectures from the state were no longer community compacts developing out of bloodline family organizations in local hamlets.

In addition to voluntary compacts, other attempts were made to use Neo-Confucian teaching to order the state. In the 750 years of Confucian society preceding the fall of the last dynasty in 1911, semi-private academies of higher education emerged to become influential places to study the classics. The general statement of moral and intellectual goals written by Zhu Xi for his White Deer Grotto Academy (discussed in chapter 2) became the template for a multitude of later academies all the way through the nineteenth century. Incoming students at each of these semi-private schools usually recopied for themselves these Neo-Confucian precepts of self-cultivation and social interaction so that they would have their own copies. The Neo-Confucian aim of learning as self-development prevailed in the curriculum, but the state did not neglect its interests either.

Both state bureaucrats and Neo-Confucian scholars were interested in promoting moral order in society, but the state's interest in Confucianism usually involved power and maintaining order, which involved controlling behavior, and which commonly recognized ethical norms helped to accomplish. From the official bureaucracy's point of view, order in society was all the clearer if it meant moral order. Many major academies were officially funded by the state during most of the final two dynasties, and those official academies were often located in centers of administration such as provincial capitals. Many other academies, however, were quasi-public, as local literati contributions were important in their budgets. Confucian academies were designed to be character-building institutions, but their potential for organized dissent made officials interested in monitoring them. And county magistrates had to maintain order.

The lowest-level administrator in most Chinese dynasties was the county magistrate, and it was common for him to be responsible for hundreds of villages in his county. (In the 1600s the average county population was around three hundred thousand.) To county magistrates, the value of a Confucian education in promoting social order was reflected in the manuals written for their use. *A Complete Book Concerning Happiness and Benevolence: A Manual for Local Magistrates in Seventeenth-Century China* is a seventeenth-century example.

> In former times department and district magistrates considered the promotion of education and economic welfare their prime responsibility. Tax collection was next in importance, followed by the administration of Justice. If education is neglected, the people will not know the principles of filial piety, brotherly love, propriety, and virtue, and all manner of antisocial and disruptive behavior

will occur. When economic welfare is overlooked, the people will find it hard to support their families and will worry about having to leave their native place to make a living elsewhere. Under such circumstances, no amount of flogging can compel them to pay their taxes. The meek will suffer in silence, while the strong will take a chance and rebel. It is obvious, therefore, that the promotion of education and economic welfare should be the first priority in local administration.[7]

Attempts to foster moral order in the state took on myriad forms, including community compacts, the role of humane elders in life-cycle rituals, and socialization of the Confucian elite in quasi-public academies. In many periods these organizations and customs were, unfortunately, manipulated to serve the more immediate needs of ruling bureaucrats. All, however, had character-building dimensions that Neo-Confucians supported. As social activists in the literate class, Neo-Confucians actively shaped local communities, kept them decentralized, and volunteered to play leadership roles in these communities.

Step Eight: Bring Peace to All

The elimination of internal strife and disunity in government is the focus of the final step in the Eight-Step program. One passage in the *Classic of Documents* often cited for this purpose criticizes high officials who were jealous of talented people and who therefore hesitated to allow their advancement: "Let me have but one minister, sincere and devoted . . . who, upon finding sage-like men, loves them in his heart more than his speech expresses, truly showing himself able to accept them."[8] This is the crux of employing self-cultivation in service to the state: to bring about peace through promoting humane civil servants. Another guideline referred to an official who learned from what he had despised when he was a subordinate. As the *Great Learning* commentator Zengzi put it, rather simply, "In leading those behind you, do not practice what you hate in those ahead of you." [9]

A good monarch was easy to describe; the *Classic of Odes* provides the text: "What the people love he loves; what the people hate he hates. This is called being father and mother to the people."[10] Zhang Zai took up this advice in *Reflections on Things at Hand.*

Please tell the officers at court: It is not enough to remonstrate with a ruler for the wrong employment of ministers or to blame him for the mistakes in government. If they can enable their ruler to love the people in the world as his infants, the virtue of his rule will be daily renewed, people presented to serve the government will be talented scholars, the way of ancient kings and emperors will be fulfilled without going astray, and both the learning of the way and the methods of government will be achieved without a divided mind. (VIII.25)

The compassion of a sage-like ruler would, ideally, reach down through all levels of the social hierarchy to the young and even orphans — in fact, to anyone not fully able to take care of him or herself. Such a ruler would also respect the elders in his family, and thus his example of filial piety would serve as a model for how elders throughout the society should be respected. To the extent that this imperial example is emulated, then, the aged population, much like orphans, would be cared for by the rest of society. Examples of this conduct in the imperial family were noticed and pointed out by officials, and Confucian analysts assumed that the reputation of such a benevolent ruler would eventually spread throughout that state. A truly compassionate monarch would not think of neglecting his own family's support, and therefore, by extension, neither would he neglect the economic well-being of the entire populace in his state — who should be conceived as related to the monarch like children to a parent. The acquisitive monarch, on the other hand, would watch idly as unity in his state, like a family in disarray, dissolved into selfishness. As Zengzi's commentary on the *Great Learning* perceptively noted, "When wealth is gathered [plundered] the people disperse; when wealth is dispersed the people gather [in trusting loyalty]."[11] The Neo-Confucians reasserted the same point with even broader implications.

Cheng Hao once had an audience with the emperor who reigned from 1068 to 1085 CE and minced no words with him: "To exercise one's selfish mind and to depend on a partial application of humanity and righteousness is the way of the despot. . . . If one pretends to be humane and righteous . . . one becomes [despite appearances] despotic. The two ways are quite different. One must clearly examine their starting point." The opposite path, Cheng pointed out, had international implications. "If Your Majesty will examine the words of ancient sages, realize that the [legendary] Way of Yao and Shun is all complete in yourself, examine yourself and be sincere, and extend this to reach all the four seas [which surround China], the next ten thousand generations will be very fortunate indeed" (*Reflections* VIII.2).

Neo-Confucians of the Song era and later believed that if a unified state emanated force of character, the surrounding peoples would treat it with trust, and no strife would be easily visited on that state. The argument presumed that the truly humane leader would naturally generate peaceful relationships with others. The tranquility of a state, according to this view, depended on the quality of the humane character emanating from its government. The humane behavior traits of a ruler who was considerate were assumed to generate friends rather than enemies, to nourish the well-being of the people, and thereby to sustain the ruler as well as his subjects.

For Zhu Xi the final three steps in the Eight-Step program encompassed the social phase. Zhu felt that these three steps implemented the dictum from the first sentence of the *Great Learning* that says "renewing the people" is a cardinal component of true learning. This idea of renewal is illustrated in the commentary on the section attributed to Zengzi, which cites passages from the *Classic of Documents* and the *Classic of Odes*. Zhu interpreted these historical references as proof of the successful self-cultivation of former kings that allowed them both victory over bad rivals and the ability to extend their virtue to the people.

PART III

Self-Cultivation Upgrades
The Fifteenth Century through the Nineteenth Century

CHAPTER 5

Reforms in Neo-Confucianism
The Fifteenth to the
Eighteenth Centuries

Chinese rule of China was restored when the Ming dynasty conquered the Mongols in 1368. In 1415 the Ming leadership published by imperial decree its own edition of Neo-Confucian interpretations of the Four Books and Five Classics, which became the standard for the Ming civil service examinations. However, the first fifty years of Ming rule brought about remarkable Neo-Confucian sacrifice. A cruel usurpation by the uncle of the second Ming emperor led to the slaughter of some forty thousand people as the uncle's dragnet for suspected dissenters swept down from Beiping (Beijing) to the southern capital in Nanjing. The future Yongle emperor falsely accused officials of turning his young nephew against the policies of the founding Ming emperor, who was the usurper's father. Yet some of these same court officials would become indispensable in validating the uncle's claims, and several turned out to be men of inviolable principle.

After the palace was burned by the uncle and the emperor presumed killed in the fire, the uncle took over the emperorship. He then sought public legitimation of his accession and turned to a prominent official named Fang Xiaoru (1357–1402), who was a former advisor to his nephew and a dedicated follower of Song Neo-Confucianism. Fang had counseled the nephew to pursue a less centralized model of government based on the Song period; he had also called for enlarging the role of scholar-officials relative to the emperor.

As the uncle took power, Fang was swept into prison by his soldiers, but he now brought Fang from his prison cell and tried to enlist his support in order to justify his attack on the nephew. However, upon Fang's questioning, the uncle's true motives were revealed when he weakly claimed that his nephew had taken his own life in the palace fire. Fang had heard earlier that another high official who had refused to validate the usurper's claims had had his tongue cut out — although he still managed to expose the usurper's treachery by writing on the floor in blood.

Even knowing this, Fang rejected the usurper's false arguments and responded with statements regarding how succession should legitimately proceed. The usurper told Fang, "My proclamation to the realm must be drafted by you, sir," and gave him a brush pen. Flinging the brush to the floor, Fang answered, "If I must die then let me die; I will not draft your proclamation."[1] Enraged, the usurper ordered Fang's death by dismemberment, as well as the extermination of Fang's living relatives to the tenth degree of blood relationship.

The Thought of Wang Yangming

In 1521 Wang Yangming, the exiled scholar of singular insight discussed in the introduction to this volume, developed a new direction in Neo-Confucian thought. After his sudden insight during his exile and during his subsequent career of leadership as both a scholar-official and general, he made public some of his suspicions regarding the doctrines of Song-period Neo-Confucians. He believed that the Cheng brothers and later Zhu Xi had left some basic insights of Confucius and Mencius behind in formulating Neo-Confucianism. Just as Lu Xiangshan had argued during the Song, for Wang and others who gradually joined his Learning of the Mind-and-Heart school, that which made a person good came not from recognizing the principle in things, but from innate knowledge (liangzhi). This position referenced the classical insights of Mencius that human beings are born with built-in capacities to be good. When apprehended, Wang further argued, these innate moral sensitivities brought about a change in one's behavior.

During the Song period Lu Xiangshan had gone so far as to state that no curriculum of texts was necessary to guide one in finding the Way. After all, the earliest primitive kingship in Chinese lore, that of the sage-kings Yao and Shun, had preceded writing altogether. Following the Ming period, the adherents of the Lu Xiangshan and Wang Yangming position (the Lu-Wang school) did not stress a detailed program of academic study, as did the more orthodox Cheng-Zhu school of Neo-Confucianism. Some of Lu's followers in the Song period, in fact, went to the extreme and pursued sudden enlightenment in Chan Buddhism — whose discipline stressed not being dependent upon the written word at all. Despite this temptation Wang condemned Chan Buddhism and had his own way of accessing innate knowledge.

Wang's position was intriguing. One's mind-and-heart is given at birth devoid of the conventional distinctions one makes in everyday social life. Serious self-cultivation through the absolute sincerity of intentions allows one to see the true character of the innate self. Because it is an act of will or intention that reveals one's inner sensibilities, this new knowledge also implies a change in one's behavior. For example, if we found ways to access commiseration in the innate physical nature of our mind-and-heart, we would begin to act with a new awareness of that capacity. Much like a pungent or sweet smell, mental knowledge of morality implies repulsion or attraction; that natural reaction determines how one will act. In short, access to one's innate knowledge means knowing becomes doing.

Wang's critique of the Cheng-Zhu position was finally articulated on paper in a radically revised way to look at the Eight-Step program found in the *Great Learning*. While Wang's rereading of the classic imposed his views rather heavily on the text, his critique began with a concern that was credible to a large number of scholars, because the original text of the Eight-Step program in the *Record of Rites* had actually begun with Zhu Xi's step three, "Make One's Intentions Sincere." It was Zhu who had revised the order so that the idea of principles metaphysically inherent in nature and in minds-and-hearts would become the first step of recognizing (investigating) things. Wang restored the original opening of the ancient text to "Make One's Intentions Sincere" in order to emphasize human intention, action, and the extension of innate knowledge.

As far as Zhu's insistence that step one be "Recognition of Things and Affairs," Wang believed it was an unwarranted addition by Zhu to begin the text and self-cultivation with a search for metaphysical principles. Instead, Wang saw the first step as correcting that which is selfish or incorrect in one's mind-and-heart (*xin*) so that one could then see its original makeup. Pure knowing in this way thus presumed that all moral principles are not independent of a person in the outside world, but are products of the mind-and-heart. Moral knowledge is ultimately innate knowledge.

Apart from these differences with Zhu, Wang's long service in public office left him quite bitter regarding the political realities that selfishness and ambition had perpetuated in the society he loved. He wrote, "For up to the present time it has been several thousand years since the poison of the doctrine of success and profit has infected the innermost recesses of the human mind, and has become our second nature. People have mutually boasted of their knowledge, crushed one another with power, rivaled each other for profit, mutually striven for superiority through skill, and attempted success through fame."[2] Wang felt the Confucian message had little chance of reversing so lamentable a record in his own lifetime. How could such a grasping society recognize the powers of innate knowledge?

Even accepting that the Confucian Way had not prevailed in Chinese history and was lost in his own day, Wang still lamented the related development that "some students turned to Buddhism and Daoism and were deceived by them." He added, "At bottom there was nothing in these systems that could overcome their desire for success and profit." Yet Wang held out hope for an eventual return of virtue to power because human nature itself is innately good, and he felt there was hope for the sage who could understand the promise of human nature. He shared a nuance about the function of humaneness that Cheng Hao and Zhang Zai had endorsed long before, in the Song period, but that Zhu Xi did not share.

> The mind of a sage regards Heaven, Earth, and all things as one body. He looks upon all people of the world, whether inside or outside his family, or whether far or near — but all with blood and breath — as his brothers and children. He wants to secure, preserve, educate and nourish all of them, so as to fulfill his desire of forming one body with all things. Now the mind of everybody is at first not different from that of the sage. Only because it is obstructed by selfishness and blocked by material desires, what was originally great becomes small and what was originally penetrating becomes obstructed.[3]

In his own Ming dynasty Wang particularly lamented that the scholarly class had turned to the literalness of "seeing and hearing," rather than actively standing up for moral government, and he also condemned academic dedication to memorization, recitation, and the indulgence in flowery compositions that got in the way of access to innate knowledge.

Explicitly populist Neo-Confucians such as He Xinyin (1517–1579) and others in the left wing of the Wang Yangming subgroup further argued that the ordinary person could find direct access to sagehood — that "simple and concise" teachings could be understood directly even by the most humble peasant. He Xinyin believed that the moral capacity of everyone in the realm could be activated by founding public schools and independent academies that were open to students from common families. His own teachings focused on "discussion" (*jiang*), the aim being to identify the intellectual quality, reciprocity of sharing, and collegial friendship among fellow learners. He wrote, "Discussion implies stimulating and, usually, amicable discourse with varying opinions offered and discussed, making learning a many-sided process in contrast to the one-sided process of the learning of the self-taught and of the master-pupil relationship."[4] While Wang's ideas spread widely, some other Neo-Confucians during the same era warned that his followers were not taking book learning seriously enough.

In the early 1600s Huang Zongxi (1610–1695), a Neo-Confucian political theorist inspired by Wang, wrote *Waiting for the Dawn: A Plan for the Prince,* and in it he proposed some solutions to the lamentable state of dynastic norms that Wang had criticized earlier. Huang had been disheartened by the corruption of the Ming dynasty that led first to his father's expulsion from officialdom and eventually to his death. His book included an indictment of official Confucian accommodation of despotic dynastic law, which had been misused to serve the clever and the powerful. Like Wang, he found that Zhu Xi's optimistic hope for the self-cultivation of emperors had proven unrealistic. Huang called for the kind of institutional restraints on despotic government that would provide conscientious and good officials with relative autonomy from the autocracy of the emperor and the inner court of obsequious officials around him. *Waiting for the Dawn* argued that the obstruction to good government — much like the selfishness that blocked innate knowledge — was due to the misuse of imperial dynastic law uniquely to serve the perpetuation of the royal family, and that impeded the work of competent and decent men who served in the name of the people as a whole.

Reexamination of the Definition of Humaneness (Ren) and the Role of Ritual

The violent end of the Ming dynasty in 1644 unveiled a historical demonstration of perfidy, hypocrisy, and the blinding appeal of force equaled only by the usurpation of the second Ming emperor by his uncle in 1402. Yet the feeling of moral retribution from the usurpation was still powerful in 1644, when the Chinese bandit, Li Zicheng, conspired with the Manchu army and successfully captured the Ming capital of Beijing. Popular legend later claimed that the bandit Li was in fact a blood descendant of the Jianwen emperor of 1402 whose body had been burned beyond recognition in the charred wreckage of the Ming palace, so a shred of doubt remained as to whether or not the Jianwen emperor had survived and gone into hiding. When the last Ming emperor, a lineal descendant of the uncle who had usurped power in 1402, hanged himself on a hill overlooking the Forbidden City palace in 1644, the popular story that even some historians had entertained — that the bandit Li was actually a disguised descendant of the murdered nephew and had pledged to avenge his uncle's treachery from some 250 years earlier — was revived. But the lessons in perfidy were actually the bandit Li's to suffer.

The relatively small Manchu military force from the northeast could not have conquered the much larger Ming state without deceiving the bandit who had helped them take the Ming capital. Before the Manchu Prince Regent, Dorgon (1612–1650), rode victoriously into Beijing, he had conspired with a Chinese general to kill his putative ally, the bandit Li, and Li's army was defeated not far from Beijing by the combined forces of that general and the Manchus. As if that were not enough, Dorgon declared himself the inheritor of Chinese legitimacy and issued a declaration outlining a Mandate of Heaven to rule based on the founding Ming emperor's statement when he overthrew the Mongols in 1368. Dorgon even dared to call his foreign Manchu dynasty the Qing, or "pure," dynasty. He argued that he had been given a moral mandate to rid Beijing of the immoral bandit Li, then claimed that his Manchu people should have this mandate to keep as leaders of all of China. For the next seven years he ran the government of the young first Manchu emperor of China who took power in 1644.

Scholars in the Qing dynasty never accepted this argument, but they did raise the bitter question of what internal weaknesses in China could have allowed these foreigners — much like their ancestors, the Jurchen, in the Song era — to again overthrow a Chinese dynasty in 1644. Some Confucian scholars accused Neo-Confucianism and the inward turn that had become the norm in Neo-Confucian education after the eleventh century. The Cheng-Zhu Learning of the Way position remained strong through the 1600s, but for many scholars the question of whether to turn away from metaphysical speculation lingered.

With the issue of whether there really were metaphysical principles in all external things in question, scholars around 1700 began new philological research into the wording of the Confucian classics. They demanded verification of all ideas attributed to the sages, and they scrutinized etymologies for key terms to ensure that those terms were not interpolations reflecting non-Confucian influences. Such rigorous new textual research succeeded in uncovering a major forgery.

The shocking forgery exposed was the venerable sixteen-word Neo-Confucian formula titled "The Counsels of the Great Yu," extracted from the Old Text chapters of the *Classic of Documents* supposedly found in the fourth century of the common era and written in characters used before 221 BCE. This particular passage, which both Zhu Xi and Wang Yangming had relied on, did justify the metaphysical claim that reality had principles in it that were quite independent of the human ability to know those principles. However, by 1745 the previously accepted Old Text chapters of the *Classic of Documents* were shown to be not so old after all — in fact, they were outright forgeries written much later. Needless to say, the shock to Neo-Confucian metaphysics was destabilizing, and textual criticism spread to other texts in the Neo-Confucian canon.

One focus of the eighteenth-century philological "housecleaning" that followed was rigorous analysis of the precise meaning of the term "humaneness," or *ren*. Scholars demonstrated that the early character for *ren* was literally composed of two pictographic components: (1) the stick figure for "person" and (2) the number two. It had been written in the following way since the unification of writing in 221 BCE: 仁.

Confucians back in Han China (202 BCE–220 CE) had acknowledged this derivation, and etymological dictionaries at the time were clear that the meaning of *ren* should be "people living together." The etymology suggested that humaneness "developed" externally through human interaction. As Ruan Yuan (1764–1849), one of the greatest Confucians who bridged the period into the nineteenth century, put it, "In all cases, *ren* must first be exhibited in personal actions before it can be observed. In addition there must be two people involved before *ren* can be seen. If a person shuts his door and lives peacefully alone, closes his eyes and sits still with a peaceful attitude, although his mind contains virtue and principle, in the end this cannot be counted for what the sagely gate called *ren*."[5] The argument from philology indicated that the gateway to sagehood was not a conception of humaneness grounded in metaphysically real "principles," or that intuition into the mind might reveal, but rather a conception that social conduct instilled. The eighteenth-century philologists cited a Han dynasty commentary on the *Analects* written by Zheng Xuan (127–200) confirming he also agreed with the newly clarified etymology of *ren*. The bare-bones meaning of humaneness was then redefined and reclaimed as deriving from the interaction of two individuals.

Eighteenth-century academies began teaching that misleading definitions of humaneness posed in the post-eleventh century era could be avoided by relying upon Han-era scholars. Philological erudition redefined humaneness as realizable only in concrete human action; humaneness meant people being mutually concerned for each other. This social dimension of *ren* made interpersonal relationships the central idea in Confucian morality.

Qing dynasty scholars attacking Neo-Confucian interpretations of the classics also replaced their predecessors' emphasis on moral principle with a reassertion of the importance of ritual propriety. Confucius himself had provided a one-sentence definition of humaneness that tied it to ritual. But that passage, 12.1 in the *Analects*, was understood by Neo-Confucian interpreters to mean, "To subdue the self [interpreted as eliminating the selfish desires of the self] and return to ritual constitutes humaneness." Zhu Xi had elaborated that there is no separate way to "return to ritual" other than "subduing the self" because what is contrary to ritual is selfishness. And further, ritual was that innate moral value — "heavenly principle in measured display" — that Zhu saw as accessed immediately when selfish desires were eliminated.[6] This interpretative commentary implied that Confucius had claimed that eliminating desires was the way to humaneness. But the philologists corrected it to read "Restraining oneself in order to return to ritual." Note that the word "restrain" was not a small change; this milder reading of "subdue," to read "restrain," actually affirmed that desires need full expression in living humanely, but with moral restraint through observing proper social norms or ritual, as a constant monitor.

Proper social norms from past traditions were understood as the place to find ritual restraint. The remaining sentences in passage 12.1 were strong advice from Confucius: "If contrary to ritual, do not look; if contrary to ritual, do not listen; if contrary to ritual, do not talk; if contrary to ritual, do not act." Hence, whether in one's own words, in what one saw, in what one heard, or in what one intentionally acted on, "restraining oneself" meant bringing oneself in line with the moral values and standards of conduct that had been tested and affirmed in past ritual practices.

Other more minor strains of Confucian thought joined the critical philologists of the eighteenth century in reconstructing the prominent position of social ritual. One such scholarly lineage that actually had its own roots in the Southern Song was the Eastern Zhejiang School of Scholarship. This added current contributed to the importance of ritual, understood as proper social usage, in keeping moral thought in conformity with past reality.

The Popularity of Xunzi

Dai Zhen (1724–1777) argued that the practice of ritual was good because it would expand our innate sense of the good. His student Ling Tingkan (1757–1809), however, changed the message: the external practice of ritual was necessary to regulate one's natural impulses that were not so obviously good at birth. This argument reopened the ancient debate between Mencius and Xunzi about whether human nature at birth was incipiently good (Mencius said "had the capacity to be good") or bad (Xunzi).

Ling Tingkan did not consider "Recognition of Things and Affairs," as the first step in an Eight-Step program, as defined by recognition of principle inherent in the natural world and human affairs; rather, it could best be revealed by analyzing the record of what rituals have been passed down, and what these rituals have taught us about human behavior. Ling even argued that the first five steps found in the *Great*

Learning required mandatory work with ritual to move from one step to the next. And in ancient China Xunzi had stood out as arguing for the essential role of ritual in moral growth.

Mid-Qing scholars who resurrected the reputation of Xunzi saw him as the authority on how ritual should reassume a central role in modernized Confucianism. Yet his popularity went even deeper. His attack on goodness in human nature was implicitly an attack on Neo-Confucian assumptions of innate goodness — which was an attack on both the Cheng-Zhu and Lu-Wang schools of Neo-Confucianism.

Confucius himself had never treated any of the five moral values — humaneness, rightness, ritual, wisdom, or sagacity — as innate. One hundred and fifty years later, however, Mencius viewed all but sagacity as at least innate capacities, and we have seen that this is one reason the Neo-Confucians were fascinated with the arguments in the *Mencius*. We now know, from the newly excavated Confucian texts, that treatises like *Five Kinds of Action*, attributed to someone in Confucius' grandson's (Zisi) generation, were connected to Mencius in a lineage of transmission. One great parallel between the two thinkers was what the author of *Five Kinds of Action* said about humaneness (*ren*) and rightness (*yi*): that as one's "outer mind" engaged in social ritual, it pulled humaneness and rightness from one's "inner mind."[7] This position resonated with the *Mencius* and with the inner orientation of the Neo-Confucians much later.

Xunzi conceived of the entire Mencian argument — if sprouts of goodness in human nature are nurtured they will become *ren* (humaneness) and *yi* (rightness) — as pulling Confucianism away from the practical concerns of bettering oneself and society. Instead, one must regulate one's inborn impulses, which are largely bad and which actually required a lifelong practice of ritual. Just as a T-square provides a ninety-degree angle for an architect designing a structure, so rituals provide stable guidance for conduct that will be morally proper. A well-ordered state based on ritual will consequently be well supported and strong.

Xunzi taught that participating in considerate activities humanizes one's emotions. Lazy or gluttonous behavior, on the other hand, can tempt everyone. Planning one's life around satisfying these pleasing but ultimately negative feelings is to invite disaster, not just for oneself but in one's relationships. Like an unused muscle, one's empathy will atrophy, and neglect will prevail, accompanied by reckless, wanton, or even vicious behavior, all in the service of immediate gratification. Conversely, observing proper social norms will allow one to find emotional recuperation in those rituals. Ritual cultivates socially positive feelings.

Xunzi openly acknowledged a transmission of ideas in his time that he identified as the Zisi-Mencius lineage, but he debunked it as making unwarranted assumptions regarding the human capacity for innate goodness. In fact, Xunzi went so far as to claim that human nature is bad (something about which Confucius had consciously preferred to remain agnostic). He felt that a new role for ritual as well as education was required because people need both in order to constrain their bad inborn impulses.

Xunzi also distinguished progressive stages of personal cultivation. A "scholar-apprentice" (*shi*) could recite the classics, while a morally exemplary person (*junzi*) who has studied the ritual texts and internalized their message has a sense of moral compass.

> Anyone who has reached the stages of the exemplary person and scholar-apprentice observes the proper degree of courtesy and obeys the rules of seniority. No improper words leave his lips; no evil sayings come from his mouth. With a benevolent mind he explains his ideas to others, with the mind of learning he listens to their words, and with a fair mind he makes his judgments. He is not moved by the censure or praise of the mob; he does not try to bewitch the ears and eyes of his observers; he does not cringe before the power and authority of eminent men; he does not feign delight in the words of the ruler's favorites. Therefore he can abide by the Way and not be of two minds, can endure hardship without betraying his ideals, and can enjoy good fortune without overstepping the bounds of good conduct. He honors what is fair and upright and despises meanness and wrangling. Such is the discourse of the exemplary person and scholar-apprentice.[8]

Moral direction from a teacher will revitalize ceremonious virtue and reauthorize moral actions. The exemplary person in Confucianism is both a teacher and a mentor.

China's final three centralized bureaucratic states, the Yuan, Ming, and Qing dynasties, all endorsed the study of Cheng-Zhu Neo-

Confucianism as the orthodox way to prepare for the civil service examinations, meaning that from the fourteenth to the twentieth centuries the Learning of the Way interpretation of the classics was officially sponsored in China. The brilliant ideas of Wang Yangming inspired many reformers during that time, but they never challenged the official Cheng-Zhu interpretation that prepared scholar-officials through the examination system. At the end of this period, in the eighteenth century, the widespread movement to reassess the meaning of the Confucian classics through philology and literary criticism redefined some Neo-Confucian interpretations of the canonical texts. But a philologically corrected Cheng-Zhu orthodoxy remained the ideological pillar supporting the dynastic state as the nineteenth-century dawned.

CHAPTER 6
The Nineteenth-Century Synthesis in Confucian Learning

In the early nineteenth century, several of the new Qing dynasty academies followed the eighteenth-century emphasis on both new textual criticism, called evidential research, and ritual in their institutional precepts and in their curricula. The Retreat for the Philological Analysis of the Classics (Hangzhou, 1801) and the Sea of Learning Academy (Canton, 1826) were two; following their model a bit later, the Dragon Gate Academy (Shanghai, 1865) and Southern Quintessence Academy (Jiangyin, 1884) were exemplars of combining philological scholarship with ritual practice. Classics were taught as historical documents, which allowed recognition of possible interpolations from much later times; such passages were scrupulously corrected. The earliest etymological dictionaries and compilations on historical phonology took on a new research value for scholars seeking the precise meaning of classical-period passages. Rigorous collation techniques reconstructed lost texts, and even pre–Qin-period texts outside the Neo-Confucian canon were allowed a restricted place in the curriculum.

At all of these institutions a significant new synthesis of Confucian scholarship occurred that can be considered the final culmination of Confucian ethics as taught and practiced in imperial times. By the mid-eighteenth century the trend in Qing scholarship to rely on Han dynasty sources was led by Hui Dong (d. 1758); his Han Learning group vigorously adopted the successful philological research techniques of the evidential research movement. By the beginning of the nineteenth century Han Learning had fully incorporated the critical scholarship of the evidential research movement while retaining its priority for Han dynasty sources. The remarkable nineteenth-century synthesis that followed combined philological erudition, often summarily termed Han Learning, with the moral cultivation of Song and Ming dynasty Neo-Confucianism usually simply termed Song Learning.

At the turn into the 1800s a host of commentaries on the *Analects* of Confucius were published that heralded the breadth of this synthesis, as illustrated by the career of Huang Shisan (1789–1862). Huang is typical of many Qing-period scholars who chose not to enter officialdom, but whose life's work set the standard for high-quality scholarship for academicians and officials alike. His personal story begins when he passed the prefectural-level Flourishing Talent civil service degree, and a few years later he was on his way to the second-level provincial examination (*xiangshi*). While he was on his way to the provincial capital where the exam was being administered, his mother succumbed to a contagious disease that had ravaged their home area, and she died. Huang was devastated and pledged filial commitment to her memory, commemorating the day of her death for the rest of his life, and he swore never to take official examinations again. He kept this commitment, dying at age seventy-four after an extremely productive scholarly life outside of officialdom.

Huang's masterwork on the *Analects* was titled *Lunyu hou'an* (The *Analects* with Comments Added); it applied rigorous philological standards to expurgate any misreadings of the passages by scholars of the Song and Ming Neo-Confucian persuasion. His methodology entailed defining each character in the sacred text; loan variants, or related terms that might be interchangeable with a character, were tested to clarify the intended meaning. Extreme care with accurate sentence divisions was essential to determine the exact meaning of passages. But Huang deeply respected the work of Zhu Xi, and his corrections were not intended as an attack of Neo-Confucianism. Indeed, in his masterwork he values Zhu's commentary equally with Zheng Xuan's commentary from the Han dynasty. Describing the mix of moral cultivation from Song learning with the philological care from Han learning that Huang demonstrated, one official who was the educational commissioner of a southern province in 1825 said, "Han Learning is like selecting rice; Song Learning is like cooking it."[1] In other words, the selection of the kind and quality of rice was the scholarly contribution provided by the philology of evidential research, or Han Learning, while the cooking of the rice's moral meaning so it could be consumed and thus nourish (the moral growth of the individual) was provided by the Song Neo-Confucian school.

At least ten serious scholarly works on the *Analects* emerged from the generation of scholars at the turn into the nineteenth century, including the incisive work of Cui Shu (1740–1816), who identified the last five books of the twenty-book *Analects* as a later layer in its composition. The most lasting scholarly annotation and commentary on the *Analects* was written by Liu Baonan (1791–1855) and finished by his son after his death — not uncommon in Chinese classical scholarship. Liu's *Correct Meaning of the "Analects"* refers the reader to Neo-Confucian readings of selected passages, but each such insight was first purified by rigorous evidential research analysis. Liu used intertextual comparison with passages from the other Four Books, as well as comparison with passages from the *Gong yang* commentary on the *Spring and Autumn Annals*. In many passages Liu refers to exposing their subtle meanings, which validated another new trend — that of viewing passages by disciples in the *Analects* as testimonials, much like the commentaries on the *Spring and Autumn Annals;* that is, as repositories of careful meanings that Confucius himself chose not to elaborate in writing.

Improved academy education after 1800 adopted the new curricular standard of paying equal attention to moral principles and philology, then syncretically mixed the two emphases. A look at academy practices in the nineteenth century reveals how the synthesis was actually implemented in Confucian education. The intellectual orientation of the synthesis was clear at the Sea of Learning Academy in Canton, founded under the patronage of the seminal scholar-official Ruan Yuan. Chen Li (1810–1882), perhaps the most impressive scholar there, dedicated his life's work to an uncompromising commitment to philological accuracy and using factual evidence to establish the meaning of passages, yet he never challenged the moral authority of the Neo-Confucian understanding of self-cultivation, and he insisted upon a balance between moral and philological emphases throughout his career. Later in the nineteenth century the model was validated when both Dragon Gate Academy and Southern Quintessence established themselves using the curriculum and the pedagogy of the Sea of Learning Academy.

Dragon Gate, established in the mid-nineteenth century, admitted about twenty-five students in residence, with an additional twenty-five commuter students. The headmaster, who was the master teacher, lived on the academy grounds; he employed one or two assistant teachers as needed. Recruitment for the headmaster position revealed much about the educational objectives of the institution. The Academy Regulations of 1870 stipulated the following traits: "Moral character, not the [examination] degree held, must be the criterion used [to select] . . . a man of the utmost integrity, and highest personal standards. . . . The mastery of materials to be taught, and his personal character must be equally exemplary." Further, "The master teacher must live in the institution and be available for discussion day and night. . . . Daily lessons and diaries must be explained in person and with evidence. If handled from far away, there will be little emotional commitment, and commitment will decrease from the students as time goes on. This is not compatible with the objectives of an academy."[2]

The regulations of the academy went on to say that every student had to keep two daily diaries: a diary of academic work completed and one of reading notes taken on the classics. With few lectures and no classroom instruction, the work diary fostered self-discipline and was used by the headmaster periodically to review the academic work covered by each student. Additionally, the diary entries needed to record what academic work was covered during four daily time units: early morning, prenoon, afternoon, and after the lamps were lit.

Significantly, the diary of reading notes was "presented," along with the work diary, every five days to the Dragon Gate headmaster. This pedagogical method was a variation on the daily study timetables used since the Song and Yuan eras in Neo-Confucian education. The headmaster was formally dressed, and the "Student [had to] stand before the teacher. When asked to sit down, the student [could] receive instruction." The Chinese terms that the student used for requesting instruction from the headmaster had their locus classicus in the *Record of Rites*, one of the original works of the Five Classics. In his personal diary of reading notes the student recorded what he had "taken away" (*xin de* 心得) from the texts he had studied, as well as questions raised by the reading. Academy regulations stipulated that "what one records must not be made up, nor should the pages be filled with tedious detail." Dragon Gate's own regulations noted that the headmaster, during these tutorials, was expected to give specific details on how the student should go about answering the questions he had written about the readings. These tutorial sessions were the heart of the pedagogy at Dragon Gate.

In addition to daily diaries, another precept of Dragon Gate Academy's curriculum reveals its explicit commitment to the mastery of Neo-Confucian texts.

> Studying should be systematic. First study the *dao* in the Four Books and in each classic; then expand your knowledge by studying all the histories, the *Zizhi Tongjian* [Comprehensive mirror for aid in government], and Master Zhu's *Gangmu* [Outline]. One can use the following compilations as ladders for assistance: the *Xiaoxue* [Elementary education]; *Jinsi lu* [Reflections on things at hand]; and various collections on nature and principle. In this way one can use understanding the subtle essence of the principles of morality (*yili*) to direct one's behavior.
>
> Selections from the hundred philosophers [and from] the classics, histories, and all related practical volumes can be studied according to the ability of the student. After that, remaining energy can be used on composition and on preparation for the civil service exams. One cannot be lazy or inconsistent; and one cannot read carelessly in a variety of books. One progresses according to one's own ability, clarifying the *ti* [substance] and attaining the *yong* [implementation]. This will lead to real benefit, and is the right way to approach study.[3]

Liu Xizai, Dragon Gate's headmaster from 1866 to 1880, reviewed the entries in the diaries of reading notes with great personal care, often working with one student after another until midnight. He reinforced whatever astute observations the student had made and corrected misunderstandings in his notes. In general, headmasters evaluated the second, or work, diaries submitted at the same time, being vigilant in discerning each student's diligence and depth of understanding. Liu embodied this care and vigilance — for fourteen consecutive years he personally supervised the progress of each of his students. After his death, articles and funerary inscriptions written by his former students testified to the remarkable lifelong student-teacher bonds that had been established.

At many of the good Confucian academies monthly essay examinations were combined with the daily diaries to complete the academy's pedagogy. Eight essays written on topics announced each month were collected from every student at the end of each academic year, and their grades were tallied; the quality of the essays was important in determining whether the student would be retained and his scholarly stipend, which covered room and board, renewed for another year.

At Southern Quintessence Academy, which adopted Dragon Gate's pedagogy when it opened in 1884, two essays a month instead of one became the norm. Significant monetary prizes were given for the top papers, and bottles of wine were given for second- and third-place monthly essay winners. Students naturally were attracted by these prizes, so the headmaster tried an experiment at the end of the 1890s: the number of essays was increased to one every ten days; however, he discovered that the additional preparation time necessary for three essays a month interfered with students' ability to keep up with in-depth diaries of reading notes. Consequently, in 1898 the number of essays was again reduced to two per month, and when this change was announced in a Shanghai newspaper, the notice from the academy stated that learning through the reading-notes diaries must not be compromised. The newspaper did not indicate that Song-period Neo-Confucian academies had first developed the pedagogical technique of reading notes in the eleventh century, but it made clear that reducing monthly essays provided more time for reading-notes entries, and that regardless of experiments or change, the diaries had proven their educational value so effectively that they had to accompany all work.

Southern Quintessence Academy's headmaster in 1898 was Huang Yizhou (1828–1899), one of the last giants in late-nineteenth-century scholarship. Like his father, Huang Shisan (the man discussed above who refused to ever retake the civil service examinations after his mother died), Huang Yizhou saw no conflict between the evidential research textual critics and the Cheng-Zhu School of Neo-Confucianism. Huang Yizhou had been trained in Han Learning at the Retreat for the Philological Analysis of the Classics in Hangzhou by the great classicist Yu Yue (1821–1907). When Huang was headmaster at Southern Quintessence Academy from 1885 to 1898, he explicitly rejected the factionalism that had separated the Han Learning and Song Learning schools during the eighteenth century. By 1864, the recent fourteen-year suppression of the populist Taiping rebels had exhausted the Qing national treasury, and the dynasty had suffered military defeat more than once at the hands of different European powers. For those academies founded later in the nineteenth century — Southern Quintessence was founded in 1884 — the future stability of the Qing dynasty was a concern, and academic in-fighting would have been a costly luxury.

Like Ruan Yuan at the beginning of the nineteenth century, Huang Yizhou celebrated the practical value of ritual. Huang asked all students at Southern Quintessence to post *Analects* 6.27 above their desks; it instructed readers to be broadly erudite in studying written texts, but then to understand those texts in light of proper social usage or ritual. This guideline hinted at the excesses of Cheng-Zhu metaphysics, or as Huang put it, "*Li* [ritual] must, of necessity, be in accord with past reality, whereas 'principle' [as emphasized by Song learning] can be just speculation."[4] Nineteenth-century Confucian academies largely retained Zhu Xi as a guide to self-cultivation, yet his metaphysics and even his quest for sagehood were often excluded from the original Neo-Confucian program. Considering the historical and political issues of the time, adhering to the hard evidence of socially grounded practice provided a compass for the present. Academy curricula in the latter part of the nineteenth century mandated analysis grounded in the realm of lived experience so that practical knowledge could be generated for the present.

In the China of 1895, the most sophisticated formulations of the true meaning of the classics combined the best Neo-Confucian analysis of the Song, Yuan, and Ming dynasties with the most searching textual critique of the Qing evidential research movement. These readings of the classics would be the last expression within the imperial state of the two-thousand-year-long evolution of the ethical tradition of self-cultivation. Qing scholarship and commentaries on the classics were still surrounded and supported by a living Confucian society in which Confucian values could be practiced, but in the national reforms between 1895 and 1911 the institutions of scholarly training, the Confucian academies, were mandated by law to convert to modern public schools. The training that had formerly focused on self-cultivation then became the preserve of new "ethics" courses in public schools, or in very rare cases were taught in isolated institutes on the periphery of twentieth-century society.

The 1911 revolution overthrew dynastic government, and with it the Neo-Confucian possibility that political authority would derive from the moral authority of officials trained in the Confucian ethical classics. In the twentieth century republican governments, first in 1912 and again in 1949 with the People's Republic, established public school systems with little place for the Confucian classics. But then, some two hundred years after the vital synthesis of Confucian schools that began around 1800, an academic revival of the Confucian tradition began again among scholars inside and outside the People's Republic of China. The academic revival of Confucianism that began in the 1990s had one obstacle, however, not present as the nineteenth century opened: there was little societal context for the practical application of those ideas in the 1990s, whether in the People's Republic of China, Singapore, Taiwan, or Hong Kong. After all, Confucius himself had said that moral and spiritual values could not be fully realized in an individual without practicing them. Around 2001 the first Neo-Confucian academy was founded precisely where the exiled Wang Yangming had experienced his deep insights at Dragon Field in China's remote hinterland. Named the Yangming Retreat (Yangming jingshe) and financed by some wealthy businessmen, it was established almost exactly one hundred years after the last classical academies were ordered eliminated in 1901. In 2007 a prominent professor at Beijing University, Zhang Xianglong, called for "preservation zones," modeled after the way the Amish lived in the United States, so that Confucian families and clans could practice family rituals apart from the pressures of modern life. His book, *Refuge of Thinking: Ancient Chinese Philosophy in the Age of Globalization,* used the parallel of preservation zones for endangered biological species and argued that conservation of Confucian practices in protected areas would demonstrate the relevance of Confucian social and political traditions to contemporary society. In the early twenty-first century academics revived Confucian social and political theory and were in search of a societal context in which the practice of Confucian values could be fostered.

Interpretations of the Classics at the
End of the Nineteenth Century

Let us look now at how Neo-Confucian self-cultivation was left for posterity at the end of the last imperial state, when the social context was more favorable to practice. Important passages from the Neo-Confucian canon are highlighted below to make clear the updated nineteenth-century synthesis of Neo-Confucian self-cultivation. The wording of each passage reflects how the orthodox Cheng-Zhu tradition would have understood that passage.

Let us first examine a passage in the *Mean* to see the difference that Han-Song syncretism made to Zhu Xi's Southern Song reading of the same passage. The beginning of chapter 13 in the *Mean,* broken into three parts, reads this way:

1. The Master said, "The Way (*Dao*) is not far from human beings. If a person in following the Way distances oneself from other people, it cannot be considered the Way."
2. The *Classic of Odes (Songs)* says,
   Hew an axe handle, hew an axe handle;
   The model is near at hand. [#158]
   > We take hold of one axe handle in order to hew another axe handle. Yet if we look from one to the other, the two appear far different. Therefore, the exemplary person uses the Way to govern men. When they are reformed, the exemplary person stops.
3. Being true to oneself (*zhong*) and empathetic toward others (*shu*) one keeps near to the Way. What one does not wish done to him he does not do unto others.

The final line recalls the same negative statement of the Golden Rule as it is stated in *Analects* 12.2 and 15.24. The interpretation of the passage for Song Neo-Confucians such as Zhu Xi, who believed that humans have an innately good nature, would be that the text says that the exemplary person (*junzi*) knows that however good an existing model of leadership is, it will not equal the perfection of the inherently good human nature all people share. The exemplary person can do his or her best to emulate that model behavior so others can witness it, and then when the community actualizes it, exemplary persons have done their jobs as good leaders.

The key revision of this way of thinking by the nineteenth-century synthesists — from Ruan Yuan at the beginning of the century to Huang Yizhou at the end — began from the position that goodness and humaneness are not innate patterns or principles in human nature waiting to be discovered or unobscured. Rather, their understanding was that humaneness develops from human nature only as one's relationships in life bring it into being. Humaneness needs to be formed, even though the capacity to develop it is available to all humans. The first line of the passage above makes this case: the *Mean* makes clear that if a person searches for the moral Way anywhere that "distances oneself from others," or separates oneself from other persons, then it cannot be considered the Way.

But Zhu had conceived of humaneness as the substance of mind, which is present at birth and has the objective reality of metaphysical principle. He saw humaneness as the pattern or principle of the mind-and-heart. How, then, does one shape morality and develop *ren,* or humaneness, according to the nineteenth-century synthesis? The line "Hew an axe handle, hew an axe handle; / The model is near at hand" above suggests that becoming a moral exemplar is possible only with social interaction. The raw material of, say, the trunk of a hickory tree that might be shaped into an axe handle can be compared to the raw material of human nature that will need to be shaped and refined to develop its humaneness. Just as the axe blade shapes a section of the trunk, so does considerate interaction with other people build one's character.

Repeating the phrase "hew an axe handle" in the poem suggests repeated shaping of the wood by the axe head. Similarly, only through continuous interactions with others can the empathetic give-and-take of putting yourself in the place of another allow you to shape morally exemplary behavior. The repeated practice of considerate human relations actually forms one's nature into the moral character possessed by an exemplary person.

In general, everyone finds it rather easy to sense whether others are treating us in a considerate way — whether they are attempting to put themselves in our place before deciding how to act toward us. This is why relationships are indispensable as a consistent means to find out how to behave respectfully. In being considerate and in being treated with consideration, reciprocity of viewpoint is the sharp edge of the axe with which one can hone one's moral behavior. Like the model axe with which one can hone one's moral behavior. Like the model axe handle, model behavior in each person is shaped more perfectly by each considerate act.

Zhu felt that humaneness lay in humans' original nature, which itself is pure, but only the mind of the Way (*Dao xin*) can recover knowledge of it. However, for Liu Baonan, the foremost nineteenth-century specialist on the *Analects* who incorporated the position of the nineteenth-century synthesis in his work, humaneness cannot be discovered or recovered from within one's innate nature. Instead, only by interacting with others can humaneness be enacted or carried out. The sharp edge of the axe of humaneness is reciprocity. One might add that the blade grips because humans are capable of some analytical reflection on their actions each day. Changing one's intentions the next day in an effort not to repeat the mistakes made today in human relations reshapes one's model behavior.

"The Foremost Passage in the *Analects*"

Zhu claimed that *Analects* 4.15 was the most important passage in the classic. Let us examine why.

> The Master said, "Can! [name of a disciple] There is a unity which interconnects my way."
> Zengzi replied, "I see."
> After the Master had gone out, one of the disciples asked, "What did he say?"
> Zengzi replied, "The way of the Master consists in nothing more than *zhong* and *shu*."

Zhu's explanation of this crucial passage derived from his philosophical position that there are metaphysical principles that inhere in all things. As far as human nature goes, he believed those innate principles can be revealed, and, in the tradition of Mencius, they will turn out to be good. Zhu assumed *zhong* is part of the inner mind, and it means "revealing one's mind fully" and therefore accessing the goodness that is there.

The psychology of these moral categories was subtle as Zhu explored how accessing innate goodness is tied to "inferring from oneself" to others, or *shu*. If one can be completely in touch with one's inner goodness, then *zhong*, that very state in which one is "being true to oneself," is achieved. Reaching that point, each person will see how extending those good feelings outward to connect to others makes reciprocity (*shu*) derivative from *zhong*. In the mind of a true sage, this interconnection will be obvious because that person will be completely in touch with his or her inner nature, or the substance, and will know just how it extends through empathy or function to other people.

But eighteenth-century evidential scholars such as Jiao Xun (1757–1809), Wang Niansun (1744–1832), and Ruan Yuan challenged Zhu's reading of the *Analects* 4.15 passage, insisting that the dispositions of *zhong* (reconceived as "balance" by the nineteenth-century reinterpretation) and *shu* (reconceived as "doing one's best for others") are tied *not* to the makeup of one's original nature, but to the way one interacts with others.

The *Mean* spoke elsewhere of "making oneself and others whole" as a definition of sincerity (*cheng*), and this was different, Liu Baonan wrote, from the Cheng-Zhu reading of sincerity as internally making oneself whole as a sage. Also, in the *Great Learning* sincere intentions (*cheng yi*) expose self-deceit and can be easily associated with the definition of sincerity in the *Mean*. Liu added that sincerity is possible only if one is balanced (*zhong*) in one's self-cultivation. Because evidential research scholars and the synthesists who followed them rendered the meaning of sincerity as "that by which one makes others whole," then sincerity was understood to carry humaneness into our behavior.[5] The focus of self-cultivation consequently turned to self-restraint and realizing sincerity in one's conduct. This redefinition of terms in *Analects* 4.15 through philology moved into the synthesist part of the nineteenth century fully in tandem with the new etymology of humaneness (*ren*) derived from Han dynasty sources as "people living together."

The Passage to Post over One's Desk

> The morally exemplary person who learns widely in the culture and keeps to the essential through ritual will surely not transgress. (*Analects* 6.27, repeated in 12.15)

For Zhu Xi, the Way was always a discovery of the invisible principles inherent in the ideal state of both things in the world and human affairs. The broad study of culture in the passage above was to apprehend those principles (*ge wu*) and extend knowledge (*zhi zhi*), as he had explained in the first two steps of the *Great Learning*. Nineteenth-century mainstream Confucian synthesizers insisted on redefining this search for moral principle in nature and human affairs. For Ling Tingkan, *ge wu* was not the recognition of principle in things, but rather the recognition of *ritual* in human affairs. Ruan Yuan followed this line of argument in noting that because humaneness has to be developed through human interaction, ritual is what actually teaches us *how to treat others* humanely.

At the end of the nineteenth century, Huang Yizhou worried that those attracted to Wang Yangming might assume that the Neo-Confucian reading of "keeping to the essential" viewed the *mind-and-heart* as the source of the essential principles explaining things, but he felt that this was speculation. The passage refers to ritual, however, which belied speculation, and that is what Huang underlined. In fact, during the thirteen years that Huang directed Southern Quintessence Academy (1885–1898), all students were asked to post the *Analects* 6.27 passage over their desks.

Huang probably would have favored Ralph Waldo Emerson's statement that related to ritual: "Manners are the happy way of doing things; each one a stroke of genius or of love, now repeated and hardened into usage."[6] Applied historically, Huang wrote that at those points in the past when conflict was rife and when *zhong* (balance) and *xin* (making good on one's word) wore thin, discussions of ritual, or proper social usage or norms, naturally emerged to facilitate human interaction. He provided examples such as the scholarly discussions that occurred at the time of the decline of the Zhou state (1045–221 BCE) and again during the debates that arose when the Jin state (265–419 CE) proved incapable of reunifying post-Han China. The decline in mutual trust so important in a stable state gave rise to debates on ritual in those periods precisely because even to initiate communication among opposing parties required more formal ceremonial or ritual language to do so.

Following his father's masterful command of the three ritual classics — the *Decorum Ritual* (*Yili*), the *Rites of Zhou* (*Zhouli*), and the *Record of Rites* (*Liji*) — Huang spent nineteen years writing a fifty-part analysis of the social and political conditions of the ancient period that discussed the norms and customs of proper social usage in the earliest ritual classics. For nineteenth-century mainstream Confucians the study of past culture became a resource not for hidden philosophic principles, but for understanding humane rituals that worked, and from which one could learn to apply humane social norms to contemporary society

It should be noted, in pointing out these differences, that Cheng-Zhu Neo-Confucians and nineteenth-century synthetic Han-Song Confucians shared a priority on consistent daily practice. The nineteenth-century mainstream interpretation would certainly have endorsed *Analects* 15.6: "When standing, see these words in front of you — 'do your utmost to make good on your word, be earnest and respectful in your conduct' — and when riding in your carriage, see them propped against the stanchion. Only then will your conduct be proper." (Today such sayings would be mounted on the dashboard of an automobile.) Zhu Xi also endorsed such daily work on self-cultivation — for example, in elucidating the revised phrase "renewing the people" in paragraph 1 of the *Great Learning,* the traditional commentary notes that Tang, the founding king of the Shang dynasty, was reputed to have had a phrase inscribed on his own bathtub to regularly remind himself to self-cultivate. It read, "If one day you truly renew yourself, day after day you should renew yourself; indeed, renew yourself every day."[7] Zhu celebrated this connection between regular physical cleansing and regular moral cleansing, but he then added the argument that accessing the goodness within one's own nature is a prerequisite to moving or influencing others. Other people would be moved to renew themselves when they observe us doing such self-renewal.

An *Analects* Passage for Advanced Learners

> Zigong said: Suppose there was one who widely bestowed benefits on the people and was capable of bringing relief to the multitude. What would you say? Could he be called humane?
>
> The Master said: Why just humane? Wouldn't he surely be a sage? Even Yao and Shun would find this difficult. Now wishing himself to be established, the humane person establishes others; and wishing himself to achieve prominence, he makes others prominent.

The ability to draw analogies from what is near at hand can be called the way to humaneness. (*Analects* 6.30)

The Neo-Confucian reading of the last lines in the above passage was discussed in chapter 2. Huang Shisan agreed with Zhu Xi that those using the "ability to draw analogies from what is near at hand" are committed to a beginning technique only, and not yet committed to humaneness itself. But from there the nineteenth-century synthesizers integrated the insights from the evidential scholars to clarify what humaneness meant and turned from analysis of the mind to the actions of the person.

Huang and his son, Huang Yizhou, insisted that humaneness is not an abstract principle in the mind, but the motivation to help others, and that it is the only way humaneness can become real. Liu Baonan applied the distinctions he had made on *Analects* 4.15 to the most intriguing part of the *Analects* 6.30 passage above. "Establishing oneself" and "achieving prominence," he argued, concern the inner balance (*zhong*) of a sincere person. "Establishing others" and "making others prominent" is a second step that goes beyond this inner work and represents *shu*, or "doing one's best for others." According to John Makeham's analysis of Liu's thought, "It is this commitment to sincerity, first awakened in regard to oneself (*zhong, cheng ji*), that enables one to recognize that the welfare of others is equally as important as one's own welfare and that, indeed, the continuation of one's own welfare depends on this recognition and so acting appropriately."[8] Both Huang Shisan and Huang Yizhou shared this understanding.

The Practice of Personal Self-Cultivation at the End of the Nineteenth Century

By the end of the nineteenth century the primary way for mainstream Confucian practitioners to self-cultivate was to work on their many personal relationships. The secondary way, through study, expanded the scope of interpersonal relationships by turning to the fund of human experience in the classics and in the histories of the past, both of which also stress the relationships of real people. Three passages from the *Analects* will specifically illustrate the high priority placed on social interaction; we can then turn to reading as a moral practice.

Social Interaction as a Moral Practice

The modern nineteenth-century student of self-cultivation might begin self-cultivation with Zengzi's three-point checklist for reflection on daily behavior (*Analects* 1.4).

> (1) Zixia said: "A person can be said to truly love learning who on a daily basis, is aware of what is yet to be learned, and who, from month to month, does not forget what has already been mastered." (*Analects* 19.5)

On the campus of the nineteenth-century residential Southern Quintessence Academy, personal conduct was part of learning. Academy regulations prohibited leaving the campus without permission and forbade visiting brothels. But rather than military-like discipline, campus culture included respectful bows every morning, not only when meeting teachers for the first time, but when meeting fellow students each day. Living on the campus became an exercise in reverent respect for one another.

> (2) [A disciple] grievingly said: "Other men all have brothers; I alone have none."
> [Another disciple said]: . . . If the exemplary person is reverent, unfailingly courteous towards others, and observant of the rites, then all within the four seas are his brothers. Why should he be distressed at having no brothers." (*Analects* 12.5)
> (3) Zigong asked: "Is there one expression that can be acted upon until the end of one's days?
> The Master replied: "There is *shu*: do not impose on others what you yourself do not want." (*Analects* 15.24)

A morally exemplary person is one who acts according to humane conduct as completely as possible, and it would take years for most students of Confucian practice to reach the exemplary stage of humaneness. Mainstream nineteenth-century Confucians stressed that relationships are the beginning and end of humane practice. It was not difficult to cite *Analects* passages like (2) and (3) above to support this position. In fact, even when Confucius described an exemplary person, the very interpersonal "making good on one's word (*xin* 信)" was the concluding step in his definition: "The Master said, 'Having a sense of appropriate conduct as one's basic disposition, developing it in observing ritual propriety, expressing it with modesty, and consummating it in making good on one's word; this then is an exemplary person'" (*Analects* 15.18).

In addition to trustworthy character, the nineteenth-century student of self-cultivation did not hesitate to use reciprocity as a lifelong method in determining what appropriate moral action toward others should be in any situation. Because the reciprocity implicit in the Golden Rule refers back to one's own interests, the Chinese Golden Rule can be easily used as a method of self-cultivation. The increasingly humane person in nineteenth-century practice fostered other interpersonal virtues that naturally elicited a similar emotion in others, such as polite and courteous behavior, consistent reverence, trustworthiness in word and deed, and interpersonal fidelity.

It is a spiritual exercise to put oneself in the place of the other person before acting; reaching out with one's heart builds one's capacity to be humane. In fact, just as physical exercise strengthens one's muscles, this spiritual exercise strengthens the heart and its capacity for compassion. After a few years of empathetic training, putting oneself in another's place becomes habitual. The mind remains the master of actions, and the objective is to make this concern for others second nature.

The social norms that communities in ancient China accepted were enshrined in their rites or ceremonies, and the ritual propriety with which they were performed was understood by Confucians to be reverent. Coming-of-age rituals and family funeral services were rites of passage that reflected these patterns of deference, and they then became conventions of civil interaction.

Quiet-Sitting. Some earlier Neo-Confucian teachers, as well as nineteenth-century synthesists, advocated quiet-sitting as one aid to self-cultivation. In 1078 CE, when Cheng Hao was appointed magistrate of a distant county, he was disappointed that the followers who accompanied him to this new post did not seem to go beyond "talking the talk" of Confucian self-cultivation: "You people accompany me here and only learn the way to talk. Therefore, in your learning, your minds and words do not correspond. Why not practice?" When the students asked what they should practice away from home, he responded, "When there is nothing to put into practice, suppose you practice quiet-sitting" (*Reflections* IV.63). In other words, Cheng's main point was to "walk the walk." Being away from relatives and their accustomed social roles, those relationships could not be maintained in practice, so the teacher suggested quiet-sitting, which is the contemplation that reduces the appeal of material gain as well as the hustle that accompanies gain, and calms the spirit to center the person for humane thinking.

It was essentially after Confucianism had responded to the popularity of Buddhism and Daoism that later Confucians added quiet-sitting as one aid in self-cultivation, but unlike Chan meditation, it was never aimed at clearing the mind of conceptual thinking. What had to accompany quiet-sitting in Confucian practice was reverence (*jing*); this idea served to humanize both public and private relationships with a sense of care and deep respect. Applied to the individual, quiet-sitting can look like meditation, and, like meditation, often even begins with the eyes closed. Obliterating the self or melding the self with greater realities, however, was never the goal. The Confucian practitioner should never lose conscious direction of the inner practice, or the goal of practicing propriety afterward. The highlighted function of reverence in Neo-Confucianism is more like concentrated awareness so that the practitioner remains always consciously respectful of others. In the eighteenth century Zhang Boxing, the editor of Zhu Xi's *Further Reflections,* was an advocate of controlled quiet-sitting. By the nineteenth century Ling Tingkan would attack Wang Yangming's definition of the phrase "even when alone, be watchful over yourself (*shen du*)," which Wang had understood as a way to experience the essence of mind. Ling argued that instead of experiencing mind, this form of reverent concern checks or monitors one's behavior to see that one's thinking is properly cultivated according to ritual.

Reading as a Moral Practice

There has probably been no other tradition so clearly committed to scholarship as the Confucian, and in the absence of sacerdotal, pastoral, or monastic activities, it was book learning and literary activity which became for the Confucian even more central tasks than for the Christian, Jew, Muslim, Hindu, or Buddhist.[9]

Confucius said he was convinced that in any town of over ten house-
holds there would be people who were more accomplished than he in
doing one's utmost on behalf of others, and better than he at making
good on their word (*xin*), but he was willing to claim that he could
be singled out as excelling on one trait: his love of learning (*Analects*
5.28). The nineteenth-century synthesis drew two conclusions. First,
it is crucial that each person take full responsibility for his or her own
moral learning. Such a commitment to full responsibility meant the
values adopted for oneself were formed independently of imposed
norms, expectations, or external pressures. Confucius felt the standards of his own day had declined so far that students of morality were
studying texts just to impress others, instead of for their own benefit.
Zhu Xi and many other Neo-Confucians of exceptional personal for-
titude taught the same point.

Second, self-cultivation necessitated becoming a self-learner for
life. Apart from doing one's utmost in existing relationships, reading was the major way to maintain a program of self-cultivation. Like
the cutting and grinding of a gem in the rough, studying the Confucian classics expanded one's constricted sphere of personal experience
to include the human experience of the morally exemplary and even
sage-like figures who wrote the ethical classics and histories.

The Cheng-Zhu Neo-Confucian sequence for study of the Four
Books remained as follows in the nineteenth century: first the *Great
Learning,* second the *Analects,* third the *Mencius,* and fourth the
Mean. And as we have seen, Zhu Xi's *Reflections on Things at Hand,*
the anthology of scholarly writings with perceptive comments on passages from all four classics, provided a useful "ladder" for the committed student/practitioner. When one finished the Four Books the
serious student then turned to the histories to read the traces of dynastic preservation and ruin, order and disorder. Once the historical
record provided the expansion of personal experience to include what
had happened in the past, one returned to a critical reading of other
philosophic thinkers of the One Hundred Schools of Thought. These
steps took a student from understanding the self, to broad learning,
and then back again to the principles of morality.

Nineteenth-century thinkers added that the main canon of texts
had to be read only in critical editions that eliminated interpretations that might have introduced the bias of non-Confucian schools
of thought, and also eliminated the metaphysical reading of passages

first imposed by Song Neo-Confucian thinkers. Nineteenth-century thinkers then gave special attention to the study of past rituals and the classics that revealed rituals. Also noteworthy is that the careful empiricism of evidential research scholars often led them to a research technique called notation books (*zhaji cezi*), which were the meticulous records of facts culled from textual criticism employing collation, etymological research, and historical phonology. One great academy headmaster, Qian Daxin (1728–1804), titled his notation books *The Record of Self-Renewal from the Ten Yokes Study*. Nineteenth-century academies taught this methodology of building knowledge, rather than trying to recover it from innate sources.

Journals. As we have seen in chapter 2, children memorized all of the Four Books and even longer classics. Selected sayings in the *Analects,* in particular, were expected to become meaningful one at a time as the life experiences of the reflective student increased. Serious student learners in the best Confucian academies would open up the full meaning of passages from the classics by submitting their diaries of reading notes to the headmaster. Many centuries after 1000 CE Confucian academy students were still composing their own diaries of reading notes; passages relevant to a student's life got priority. The practice of writing down what they took away from the passages, which crystallized their understanding in their own words, was quite similar to the scholarly skill of glossing the passages of a classic (*xungu*), the heart of ancient commentarial reasoning.

By the time such a student became a scholar-official, it was not uncommon for him to keep a daily personal diary of self-criticism as a way to comment on his personal relationships. When moral temptations or lusts crossed the minds of high officials, they would copy guiding maxims in their self-cultivation diaries — often quotations from the classics — to address such weaknesses in themselves. By the time of the Qing dynasty, as Hellmut Wilhelm has determined, "It became the custom to show these self-revealing diaries around among friends and have them add their own criticism to one's own." Within a coterie of three to five intimate friends, one would invite marginal comments on one's acknowledged weaknesses. Even the highest officials often used this regular method of self-cultivation. Reading the marginal comments of someone one trusts who is also trying to be a good person can rectify one's behavior in a reciprocal manner. The daily diaries of several powerful officials are still preserved in the Chinese record today.

One such journal belonged to Zeng Guofan (1811–1872), the governor-general who oversaw three major provinces after he led the repression of the Taiping Rebellion in 1864. Zeng argued, like Ling Tingkan, that rituals should accompany all steps in the Eight-Step program of the *Great Learning*. He recorded what his teacher, Tang Jian (1789–1872), had told him of the diary of a fellow student, Woren (1804–1871), who by then had become a grand secretary in the capital: "My teacher said, 'In recent years, Woren has been the most dedicated one. Every day he records each word he said, each move he made, and even each meal he ate. He also records his bad behavior, and the lusts he fails to overcome.'"[10]

Zeng's teacher also extracted some useful points from his own diary of introspection and self-criticism and included them in a handbook of sayings on personal cultivation. Such a book could then be studied by Tang Jian's students even after his death, and in turn by their students. Excerpts included the following.

> (1) In matters of merit and reputation you may give in to people; in matters of morals you may not. In matters of gain and loss you may obey orders; in matters of right and wrong you may not.
>
> (2) If you know yourself and know people, humaneness and indulgence will come naturally. If you do away with your ego and do away with things, "voidness" and justice will come naturally.[11]

Similarly, as discussed in chapter 3, Liu Xizai, the headmaster of Dragon Gate Academy from 1866 to 1880, titled his booklet of sayings for future students *Lessons on Maintaining Resolve*.

The Confucian synthesis of the second half of the nineteenth century concluded the self-cultivation tradition of dynastic China that had evolved since the inception of Neo-Confucianism in the eleventh century. The last great classical academy to be founded in the nineteenth century, Southern Quintessence in Jiangsu Province, took its name from Zhu Xi's Song-era visit near the location of the academy, during which he commemorated a shrine to Yan Ziyou, the only immediate disciple of Confucius who had been born south of the Yangzi River, and used the term "Southern Quintessence" in his commemorative tablet. The new academy's curriculum mandated all entering students to write a copy of the academy precepts to guide their three years of study, including the following: "It is held that the essay and other minor Confucian genres do not reveal the Way. When Zhongni [Confucius] passed away, the subtle and profound language [of the Way] was interrupted. The masters of the Northern Song were again able to transmit it. The most accomplished single person to do this was Xin'an [Zhu Xi]."[12] At the end of the nineteenth century it is clear that Cheng-Zhu Neo-Confucianism was synthesized with later trends of textual criticism, but remained very much the heart of a modernized Confucian self-cultivation practice.

Legacies

The late nineteenth-century synthesis of the Confucian ethical tradition was the tip of an iceberg, the base of which extended to before 500 BCE, when Confucius first began teaching. The nineteenth-century revision had Neo-Confucian content at its core but relied on revised texts whose wording had met the test of philological scrutiny. Some sources held dear by the early Neo-Confucians had even been exposed as forgeries. The final formulation of Confucian ethics before the empire ended in 1911 was not the pure eleventh-century Neo-Confucian formulation, but a synthesis with it.

That synthesis explained that instead of humaneness being recovered from its innate source within human nature, external relationships were built into humaneness. The objective of Song Neo-Confucians and Qing philologists had always been the same: how to achieve humaneness in one's behavior. Selecting early-ripening strains of rice so that one could double-crop the harvests required the applied science of philology. But the only way authenticated classical texts could be morally and spiritually nourishing was to cook the rice of moral growth with self-cultivation. As Cheng Yi stated long before, when he explored spiritual nourishment with metaphor: "Drink, food, and clothing serve to nourish one's body. Disposition, appearance, and conduct according to rightness serve to nourish one's virtue. And extending one's virtue to others serves to nourish mankind [in the sense of human nature]" (*Reflections* IV.3).

During the early Song dynasty the Neo-Confucian Zhou Dunyi clarified the stages of spiritual development that a serious practitioner could reach. Zhu Xi selected the following statement of Zhou to open the "Essentials of Learning" chapter in the Neo-Confucian anthology, *Reflections on Things at Hand*: "The sage aspires to become Heaven, the worthy (*xian*) aspires to become a sage, and the scholar-apprentice (*shi*) aspires to become a worthy" (II.1). The early Neo-Confucians agreed that someone who had nothing contrary to humaneness in his or her heart for three consecutive months had reached the status of a worthy. Yan Hui, long revered as the most accomplished immediate disciple of Confucius, realized this level of self-cultivation, and along with Mencius he was considered by Neo-Confucians second only to Confucius on the path toward sagehood.

In the final chapter of *Reflections on Things at Hand,* Zhu chose to end the anthology by describing the dispositions of worthies and sages such as Confucius, Yan Hui, Zengzi, Zisi, Xunzi, Dong Zhongshu, Han Yu, Zhou

Dunyi, Cheng Hao, and Zhang Zai. The exemplars of Neo-Confucianism whom we have seen take their stands in this book followed those models as they responded to crises with extraordinary moral courage. Fang Xiaoru's martyrdom in opposing the imperial usurpation of 1402 paralleled the moral indignation shown by Zhu Xi himself for corruption throughout the twelfth century. The justice demanded by Wang Yangming in the sixteenth century led to his exile, which nearly proved deadly. The reasons for the political collapse of the Ming dynasty were harshly criticized by Huang Zongxi in a work that could be published only after his death. And the moral crisis of the Taiping Rebellion in mid-nineteenth-century China drew Zeng Guofan to leadership — he who had rigorously examined his daily behavior by sharing his intimate diary with a coterie of other high officials. Accepting the moral charge of living a principled life, these Neo-Confucians themselves became moral models.

The radical redefinition of *ren,* or humaneness, during the eighteenth-century era of textual criticism was a major change both conceptually and practically. Whereas Zhu had conceived of humaneness as an innate principle of one's mind-and-heart, or "that whereby one maintains the integrity of the character of the mind," Ruan Yuan, in the eighteenth century, agreed with China's earliest etymological dictionary, which glossed the Chinese character as "people living together."

So pedestrian an etymology had major ramifications. Han dynasty scholar Zheng Xuan's influential commentary on the *Analects,* written before 200 CE, helped confirm Ruan's eighteenth-century conception of *ren.* Along with humaneness, other moral values such as empathy, tolerance, reverence, courtesy, doing one's utmost in relationships, reciprocity (*shu*), ritualized propriety, and even the mutuality of respect inherent in the exemplary person (*junzi*) are defined through social interaction; they emerge not because we can recover, through excavation, virtues inherent in human nature, but because human beings are social animals whose moral lives develop through relationships.

As metaphysics receded from the high tide of its influence, the reshaped canon of texts and particularly the mountain of literature on Neo-Confucian self-cultivation were exposed all the more prominently. The actual practice of deciding how to treat others in relationships was then understood as what makes the moral path an option in one's life. People can find a moral plane on which to conduct their everyday affairs when they learn to discipline the brutish instincts Xunzi said were part of human nature, and this moral plane becomes visible through living by considerate interactions with others.

Does Neo-Confucian self-cultivation remain a relevant resource for society in the twenty-first century? In 1993 the American cultural critic and poet Robert Bly addressed a problem he felt the United States and China shared when he spoke of the need for alternative resources to promote civility: "During the period when Mao, through the Red Guards, actively ordered citizens in China to throw away discrimination and indulge denunciation, violence, destruction of treasures, and the beating of cultural persons, increased shootings, murders, dismemberments, revenge, and mindless killings were being shown on family television in the United States."[1] Bly further complained that traditional social and moral controls in both East and West had been abandoned for ineffective attempts in the family and school to dampen the aggressive drive in children by using taboos, rules, and parental tyranny. As the constraints of commonly accepted social norms weaken in modern industrial society, one of the few places to turn for civil conduct is self-restraint through personal self-cultivation. Much more so than Chinese Buddhism or Daoism, the literature of Confucian ethics provides a storehouse of insights for the practice of civility. Mencius, in ancient China, seemed to anticipate what was coming; it is as if he were writing for future corporate CEOs in prison or elected officials who resign in shame when he said, "There are Heavenly honors, and there are human honors. Humaneness, rightness, devotion, faithfulness, delighting in goodness without tiring — these are Heavenly honors. Being a duke, High Minister, or Chief Counselor — these are human honors. The ancients cultivated Heavenly honors, and human honors followed upon them. Nowadays, people cultivate Heavenly honors because they want human honors. So when they have obtained the human honors, they cast away the Heavenly honors. This is the extreme of confusion! In the end they will lose everything" (*Mencius* 6A16).

Neo-Confucianism is primarily a moral and spiritual practice. Its doctrines unequivocally uphold the role of reverence in moral and spiritual life, just as Christianity, Islam, and Judaism do. The Neo-Confucian program for lifelong self-cultivation in this world makes reverence indispensable at every step of moral development. It begins in an empathy that reaches beyond one's family and expands by observing civility in all of one's relationships. Neo-Confucian ethics ends with a lived commitment to humaneness and moral self-restraint that sets a high standard for any society. For a Confucian practitioner the first step in correcting the moral imbalance around one is not pressing one's morality upon others, but practicing humane living through considerate relationships with others.

Such a pragmatic approach may strike the reader as strangely modern in not presuming a ready-made essential truth that one has to believe to become a Confucian, but the Neo-Confucian self-cultivation program involves no creeds, statements of belief, or even supernatural authority. Rather than stemming from a universal truth, humaneness develops and flourishes only if used. Social interaction then becomes the proper place to exercise and strengthen one's heart muscle. The more one puts oneself in the place of another, the stronger one's empathy, and ultimately humaneness, becomes.

Take away from this book the realization that an ethical tradition exists on the planet that in its last synthesis within the dynastic tradition might be called "relationship ethics." It affirms that the values held by each person take root and grow through his or her inherently relational childhood and youthful experiences. Once one has reached beyond family members and expanded the range of social interaction in nonselfish behavior, mutual caring becomes trust in social relationships. Human morality builds only through the hard exercise of interpersonal work. Neo-Confucians admired Hui, the favorite disciple of Confucius who succeeded in making humaneness a host and master within himself; nothing contrary to humaneness entered his mind for three months at a time. Beyond such a high level of personal perfection, we have the words of Confucius himself, who by age seventy no longer had to think about what moral choice to make, but simply did it. Confucius was then so completely transformed that he was humaneness.

Appendix
Chronology of Works and Thinkers with the Sequence for Reading the Four Books Indicated

The Four Books (all dates are BCE)

1045   Founding of the Zhou dynasty in ancient China

551–479   Confucius
          (2) *Analects*

d. 402   Zisi, grandson of Confucius, begins a school that later was credited, by tradition, with composing the *Mean.*

d. 290   Mencius
          (3) *Mencius*

ca. 100   The Han dynasty stretches the personal ethics of Confucius to become the official political philosophy of the imperial state. The *Record of Rites* is compiled and had chapter 42 as the (1) *Great Learning,* and chapter 31 as the (4) *Mean.*

Neo-Confucian Thinkers (all dates are CE)

Cheng-Zhu Learning of the Way (Daoxue) School
of Neo-Confucianism

    1032–1085   Cheng Hao
    1033–1107   Cheng Yi
    1130–1200   Zhu Xi

Other Neo-Confucians

    1017–1073   Zhou Dunyi
    1020–1077   Zhang Zai
    1139–1193   Lu Xiangshan
    1472–1529   Wang Yangming has reservations about Zhu Xi's interpretation of Confucianism quite similar to Lu Xiangshan's earlier reservations. This alternative Neo-Confucian position was called the Lu-Wang school.

Han-Song Synthesis

1764–1849	Ruan Yuan
1789–1862	Huang Shisan
1810–1882	Chen Li
1811–1872	Zeng Guofan
1828–1899	Huang Yizhou

Notes

Introduction

1. Adapted from Wm. Theodore de Bary and Irene Bloom, comps., *Sources of Chinese Tradition: From Earliest Times to 1600,* vol. 1, 2nd ed. (New York: Columbia University Press, 1999), 331.

2. Wm. Theodore de Bary, Carol Gluck, and Arthur F. Tiedemann, comps., *Sources of Japanese Tradition: 1600–2000,* vol. 1, 2nd ed. (New York: Columbia University Press, 2005), 260.

Chapter 1: Song Dynasty Neo-Confucianism

1. Adapted from Wm. Theodore de Bary and Irene Bloom, comps., *Sources of Chinese Tradition: From Earliest Times to 1600,* vol. 1, 2nd ed. (New York: Columbia University Press, 1999), 760.

2. Ibid., 724.

3. Mark Csikszentmihalyi, *Material Virtue Ethics and the Body in Early China* (Leiden: Brill, 2004), 299.

Chapter 2: Neo-Confucian Education

1. Wm. Theodore de Bary and Irene Bloom, comps., *Sources of Chinese Tradition: From Earliest Times to 1600,* vol. 1, 2nd ed. (New York: Columbia University Press, 1999), 743.

2. Hoyt Tillman, "Either Self-Realization or Transmission of Received Wisdom in Confucian Education: An Inquiry into Lü Zuqian's and Zhu Xi's Constructions for Student Learning," in *Educations and Their Purposes: A Conversation among Cultures,* ed. Roger T. Ames and Peter D. Hershock (Honolulu: University of Hawai'i Press, 2008), 274.

3. De Bary and Bloom, *Sources of Chinese Tradition,* 805.

4. Daniel K. Gardner, trans., *Learning to Be a Sage: Selections from the Conversations of Master Chu, Arranged Topically* (Berkeley: University of California Press, 1990), 139.

5. Daniel K. Gardner, *Zhu Xi's Reading of the "Analects": Canon, Commentary, and the Classical Tradition* (New York: Columbia University Press, 2003), 135.

6. De Bary and Bloom, *Sources of Chinese Tradition,* 834.

Chapter 3: The First Five Steps of Personal Cultivation

1. Wm. Theodore de Bary and Irene Bloom, *Sources of Chinese Tradition: From Earliest Times to 1600*, vol. 1, 2nd ed. (New York: Columbia University Press, 1999), 725–728; and Daniel K. Gardner, *Chu Hsi and the "Ta-hsueh": Neo-Confucian Reflection on the Confucian Canon* (Cambridge, Mass.: Council on East Asian Studies, Harvard University, 1986), 94.

2. De Bary and Bloom, *Sources of Chinese Tradition*, 723–724.

3. Adapted from Allen Wittenborn, trans., *Further Reflections on Things at Hand: A Reader, Chu Hsi*, compiled by Zhang Boxing (New York: University Press of America, 1991), 87.

4. Daniel K. Gardner, trans., *Learning to Be a Sage: Conversations of Master Chu, Arranged Topically* (Berkeley: University of California Press, 1990), 5.68, p. 161.

5. De Bary and Bloom, *Sources of Chinese Tradition*, 729.

6. Wittenborn, *Further Reflections on Things at Hand*, 200–201.

7. Gardner, *Chu Hsi and the "Ta-hsueh,"* 105, n. 106. See also Wittenborn, *Further Reflections on Things at Hand*, 99.

8. Wittenborn, *Further Reflections on Things at Hand*, 100.

9. Gardner, *Chu Hsi and the "Ta-hsueh,"* 108–109, n.116; emphasis added.

10. Ibid., 108.

11. Ibid., 100.

12. Ibid., 100.

13. De Bary and Bloom, *Sources of Chinese Tradition*, 683–684.

Chapter 4: The Three Steps of Social Development

1. *Zhuzi yulei* (Classified conversations of Master Zhu) (Beijing: Zhanghua Shuju, 1994), 4:1230.

2. Theresa Kelleher, "Back to Basics: Chu Hsi's *Elementary Learning (Hsiao-hsueh)*," in Wm. Theodore de Bary et al., eds., *Neo-Confucian Education: The Formative Stage* (Berkeley: University of California Press, 1989), citing "Questions of Aigong," in James Legge, trans., *Li Chi: Book of Rites*, Ch'u Chai et. al., eds. Reprint (New York: University Books, 1967), 2:266.

3. Ibid., citing *The Classic of Filial Piety*, trans. Lelia Markra (New York: St. John's University, 1961), 31.

4. *Chu Hsi's "Family Rituals": A Twelfth-Century Chinese Manual for the Performance of Cappings, Weddings, Funerals, and Ancestral Rites*, trans. and with annotation by Patricia Ebrey (Princeton, N.J.: Princeton University Press, 1991), 40–44.

5. Allen Wittenborn, trans., *Further Reflections on Things at Hand: A Reader, Chu Hsi*. Compiled by Zhang Boxing (New York: University Press of America, 1991), 147.

6. Wm. Theodore de Bary and Irene Bloom, *Sources of Chinese Tradition: From Earliest Times to 1600*, vol. 1, 2nd ed. (New York: Columbia University Press, 1999), 790.

7. Huang Liu-hung, *A Complete Book Concerning Happiness and Benevolence: "Fu-hui ch'üan-shu," A Manual for Local Magistrates in Seventeenth-Century China*, trans. and ed. by Djang Chu (Tucson: University of Arizona, 1984), 525.

8. Daniel K. Gardner, *Chu Hsi and the "Ta-hsueh": Neo-Confucian Reflection on the Confucian Canon* (Cambridge, Mass.: Council on East Asian Studies, Harvard University, 1986), 49.

9. Ibid., 114.

10. Ibid., 115.

11. Ibid., 117.

Chapter 5: Reforms in Neo-Confucianism

1. F. W. Mote, *Imperial China 900–1800* (Cambridge, Mass.: Harvard University Press, 1999), 589.

2. Wang Yang-ming, *Instructions for Practical Living and Other Neo-Confucian Writings*, trans. Wing-tsit Chan (New York: Columbia University Press, 1963), 123.

3. Ibid., 118.

4. Ronald Dimberg, *The Sage and Society: The Life and Thought of Ho Hsin-yin* (Honolulu: Society for Asian and Comparative Philosophy, University Press of Hawai'i, 1974), 90–91.

5. Benjamin Elman, "The Revaluation of Benevolence (*Jen*) in Ch'ing Dynasty Evidential Research," in *Cosmology, Ontology, and Human Efficacy: Essays in Chinese Thought*, ed. Richard J. Smith and D. W. Y. Kwok (Honolulu: University of Hawai'i Press, 1993), 66.

6. Daniel K. Gardner, *Zhu Xi's Reading of the "Analects": Canon, Commentary, and the Classical Tradition* (New York: Columbia University Press, 2003), 80–84.

7. Mark Csikszentmihalyi, *Material Virtue Ethics and the Body in Early China* (Leiden: Brill, 2004), 178–179.

8. Burton Watson, trans., *Hsun Tzu: Basic Writings* (New York: Columbia University Press, 1963), 148–149.

Chapter 6: The Nineteenth-Century
Synthesis in Confucian Learning

1. See Steven B. Miles, *The Sea of Learning: Mobility and Identity in Nineteenth-Century Guangzhou* (Cambridge, Mass.: Harvard University Asia Center, 2006), 223.

2. See Barry Keenan, "Revitalizing Liberal Learning: The Chinese Way," *Change: The Magazine of Higher Learning* 30, no. 6 (November/December 1998): 41.

3. See Barry C. Keenan, *Imperial China's Last Classical Academies: Social Change in the Lower Yangzi, 1864–1911* (Berkeley: Institute of East Asian Studies, University of California, 1994), 53.

4. Ibid., 88.

5. See John Makeham, *Transmitters and Creators: Chinese Commentators and Commentaries on the* Analects (Cambridge, Mass.: Harvard University Asia Center, 2003), 297–299.

6. See P. M. Forni, *Choosing Civility: Twenty-Five Rules of Considerate Conduct* (New York: St. Martin's Griffin, 2002), 11.

7. Daniel K. Gardner, *Chu Hsi and the "Ta-hsueh": Neo-Confucian Reflection on the Confucian Canon* (Cambridge, Mass.: Council on East Asian Studies, Harvard University, 1986), 96.

8. Makeham, *Transmitters and Creators,* 298.

9. Wm. Theodore de Bary, *The Liberal Tradition in China* (New York: Columbia University Press, 1983), 59.

10. See Andrew Cheng-kuang Hsieh, "Tseng Kuo-fan, A Nineteenth-Century Confucian General," Ph.D. dissertation, Yale University, 1975, 26.

11. Hellmut Wilhelm, "Chinese Confucianism on the Eve of the Great Encounter," in *Changing Japanese Attitudes toward Modernization,* ed. Marius Jansen (Princeton, N.J.: Princeton University Press, 1965), 300.

12. Keenan, *Imperial China's Last Classical Academies,* 91.

Legacies

1. Robert Bly, ed., *The Darkness around Us Is Deep: Selected Poems of William Stafford* (New York: HarperPerennial, 1993), xxi.

Further Readings

Readers who wish to see how inspiring Neo-Confucian self-cultivation writing can be will enjoy Zhu Xi's anthology. See Chu Hsi and Lü Tsu-ch'ien, comps., *Reflections on Things at Hand: The Neo-Confucian Anthology*, translated by Wing-tsit Chan (New York: Columbia University Press, 1967). The same fourteen categories Zhu Xi used to organize the passages from the Five Masters were applied to his own writings in the eighteenth century; see Allen Wittenborn, trans. (with commentary), *Further Reflections on Things at Hand: A Reader, Chu Hsi*. Compiled by Zhang Boxing (New York: University Press of America, 1991). My quotation of Wittenborn's passages will adapt selected terms for consistency with terminology used throughout this book.

The Four Books

The best introduction to Zhu Xi's Four Books is a paperback by Daniel K. Gardner, *The Four Books: The Basic Teachings of the Later Confucian Tradition* (Indianapolis: Hackett, 2007). Gardner discusses Zhu Xi's commentaries and uses authoritative expertise to select the poignant passages from the *Analects* and the *Mencius* to translate. This edition includes the complete text of the *Great Learning* and the *Mean*.

The earliest scholarly translation of all of the Four Books includes the Chinese text and was made by the British missionary to China, James Legge, in 1894. Legge offers useful indices of subjects treated in each work and helpful content footnotes explaining his choice of terms for each passage of English translation. See the first two volumes of James Legge, *The Chinese Classics*, rev. ed., 5 vols. (Hong Kong: Hong Kong University Press, 1960).

Selections from all four are introduced and translated in Wm. Theodore de Bary and Irene Bloom, *Sources of Chinese Tradition: From Earliest Times to 1600*, vol. 1, 2nd ed. (New York: Columbia University Press, 1999). The materials on Zhu Xi and other Neo-Confucians in this anthology are beautifully placed in their historical and educational contexts.

THE *GREAT LEARNING*

An authoritative translation of the *Great Learning* is by Daniel K. Gardner, *Chu Hsi and the "Ta-hsueh": Neo-Confucian Reflection on the Confucian Canon* (Cambridge, Mass.: Council on East Asian Studies, Harvard University, 1986). A provocative translation can be found in Andrew Plaks, trans.,

"Ta Hsueh" and "Chung Yung" (The Highest Order of Cultivation and *On the Practice of the Mean)* (New York: Penguin, 2003).

THE *ANALECTS*

On the *Analects* in English I have consistently cited Roger T. Ames and Henry Rosemont, Jr., trans., *The "Analects" of Confucius: A Philosophical Translation* (New York: Ballantine, 1998), unless otherwise indicated. Wherever Zhu Xi's wording and interpretation were at issue, I have used the *Analects* wording as Zhu Xi understood it from Daniel K. Gardner, *Zhu Xi's Reading of the "Analects": Canon, Commentary, and the Classical Tradition* (New York: Columbia University Press, 2003). Two other recent translations of value are Burton Watson, trans., *The "Analects" of Confucius* (New York: Columbia University Press, 2007), and Simon Leys, trans., *The "Analects" of Confucius* (New York: W. W. Norton, 1997). In addition, a careful piece of scholarship with selections from the long commentarial tradition of analyzing the passages can be found in Edward Slingerland, trans., *Confucius "Analects": With Selections from Traditional Commentaries* (Indianapolis: Hackett, 2003), and the Sinologist's dream is the translation and dating of sections by E. Bruce Brooks and A. Taeko Brooks, trans., *The Original "Analects": Sayings of Confucius and His Successors* (New York: Columbia University Press, 1998).

THE *MENCIUS*

A valuable translation is Bryan W. Van Norden, trans. (with introduction and notes), *Mengzi: With Selections from Traditional Commentaries* (Indianapolis: Hackett, 2008). I have cited this translation throughout the text. The *Mencius* also reads easily in D. C. Lau, trans., *Mencius*, rev. ed. (New York: Penguin, 2003). A perceptive secondary work is available from Kwong-loi Shun, *Mencius and Early Chinese Thought* (Stanford, Calif.: Stanford University Press, 2000).

THE *MEAN*

A thoughtful translation of this work by two philosophers committed to the classical period includes the Chinese text: Roger T. Ames and David L. Hall, trans., *Focusing the Familiar: A Translation and Philosophical Interpretation of the "Zhongyong"* (Honolulu: University of Hawai'i Press, 2001). All translations that I cite are from this edition. See also the combined edition with the *Great Learning*: Andrew Plaks, trans., *"Ta-Hsueh" and "Chung Yung" (The Highest Order of Cultivation* and *On the Practice of the Mean)* (New York: Penguin, 2003).

OTHER CLASSICS

The newly excavated *Wuxing* (Five kinds of action) text has been translated in a scholarly edition by Mark Csikszentmihalyi, trans., *Material Virtue: Eth-*

ics and the Body in Early China (Leiden: Brill, 2004). Quotations of the *Wu-xing* in this book come from that edition. The *Classic of Odes* is accessible in Arthur Waley, trans., and Joseph R. Allen, ed. and trans., *The Book of Songs* (New York: Grove Press, 1996). For the *Record of Rites* see James Legge, trans., *"Li Chi": Book of Rites,* edited by Ch'u Chai and Winberg Chai. 2 vols. (New Hyde Park, N.Y.: University Books, 1967). For the *Xiaojing,* see Roger T. Ames and Henry Rosemont, Jr., trans., *The Chinese Classic of Family Reverence: A Philosophical Translation of the "Xiaojing"* (Honolulu: University of Hawai'i Press, 2009).

Zhu Xi's discussions with colleagues and students compose an eight-volume modern set in Chinese. A very readable paperback edition of excerpts on important themes from some chapters is Daniel K. Gardner, trans. (with a commentary), *Learning to Be a Sage: Conversations of Master Chu, Arranged Topically* (Berkeley: University of California Press, 1990). On Wang Yang-ming, a fine translation of his writings is available in Wing-tsit Chan, trans., *Instructions for Practical Living and Other Neo-Confucian Writings* (New York: Columbia University Press, 1963). In addition, see the same author's essays in *Chu Hsi: New Studies* (Honolulu: University of Hawai'i Press, 1989), some of which relate nicely to Wang's thought as well. A clear introduction placing Wang in the classical tradition can be found in Philip J. Ivanhoe, *Ethics in the Confucian Tradition: The Thought of Mengzi and Wang Yangming,* 2nd ed. (Indianapolis: Hackett, 2002). The seminal work of Tu Weiming is accessible in his collections of essays: *Humanity and Self-Cultivation: Essays in Confucian Thought* (Berkeley: Asian Humanities Press, 1979), and *Confucian Thought: Selfhood as Creative Transformation* (Albany: State University of New York Press, 1985), as well as in his study of the *Mean* titled *Centrality and Commonality: An Essay on Confucian Religiousness* (Albany: State University of New York Press, 1989).

An introduction to the Five Classics is available in Michael Nylan, *The Five "Confucian" Classics* (New Haven, Conn.: Yale University Press, 2001). The political journey and thought of Confucius himself come alive for the modern reader in Annping Chin, *Authentic Confucius: A Life of Thought and Politics* (New York: Scribner, 2007). On Xunzi, a nice paperback translation with topical themes is easily accessible in Burton Watson, trans., *Hsun Tzu: Basic Writings* (New York: Columbia University Press, 1996). The complete works of Xunzi appear in John Knoblock, ed. and trans., *Xunzi: A Translation and Study of the Complete Works.* 3 vols. (Stanford, Calif.: Stanford University Press, 1988–1994).

Commentaries and Writings on the Neo-Confucians

The tradition of reasoning through commentaries on passages from classics was the primary technique of philosophic analysis in the Chinese tradition until modern times. Two volumes analyze the *Analects* commentaries and present to the reader how commentaries worked. The prolific scholar John Makeham translated four commentators from different eras on the *Analects* text in *Transmitters and Creators: Chinese Commentators and Commentaries on the "Analects"* (Cambridge, Mass.: Harvard University Asia Center, 2003). This volume contains unprecedented scholarship of high value. In the same year there appeared another study of Zhu Xi's commentaries by Daniel K. Gardner that has been mentioned already under the *Analects*. The two treatments overlap on Zhu Xi's scholarship and are mutually beneficial to the serious student.

Almost everything written or edited by Wm. Theodore de Bary bears on the themes I have addressed. Of particular interest will be *Waiting for the Dawn: A Plan for the Prince: Huang Tsung-hsi's "Ming-i-dai-fang lu"* (New York: Columbia University Press, 1993); note especially the introductory essay. See also his *Neo-Confucian Orthodoxy and the Learning of the Mind-and-Heart* (New York: Columbia University Press, 1981). An edited volume by Wm. Theodore de Bary and John W. Chaffee, *Neo-Confucian Education: The Formative Stage* (Berkeley: University of California Press, 1989), contains essays by other scholars on community compacts and Zhu Xi's *Elementary Learning.*

On women and Chinese Neo-Confucianism, the best place to start is Patricia Buckley Ebrey, *The Inner Quarters: Marriage and the Lives of Chinese Women in the Sung Period* (Berkeley: University of California Press, 1993). The section of the second edition of de Bary and Bloom's *Sources on Chinese Tradition* on "Women's Education," by Theresa Kelleher, contains the document by Empress Xu that I cite on women's education. See also Bettine Birge, *Women, Property, and Confucian Reaction in Sung and Yuan China (960–1368)* (New York: Cambridge University Press, 2002), as well as Chenyang Li, ed., *The Sage and the Second Sex: Confucianism, Ethics, and Gender* (Chicago: Open Court, 2000).

For a comprehensive synthesis and perceptive analysis of the Neo-Confucians as an intellectual and a political movement, and for Hu Anguo's commentary on the *Spring and Autumn Annals,* turn to Peter K. Bol, *Neo-Confucianism in History* (Cambridge, Mass.: Harvard University Asia Center, 2008). For Ming Neo-Confucianism, see Willard Peterson, "Confucian Learning in Late Ming Thought," in *The Cambridge History of China: Volume 8, The Ming Dynasty, 1368–1644, Part 2,* edited by Denis Twitchett and Frederick W. Mote (Cambridge: Cambridge University Press, 1998). A philosophically astute and readable introduction to the Chinese ethical tradition can be found in the analyses of representative figures by Philip J. Ivanhoe, *Confucian Moral Self Cultivation,* 2nd ed. (Indianapolis: Hackett, 2000). Benjamin Elman has written the authoritative study of the evidential research movement: *From Philosophy to Philology: Intellectual and Social Aspects of Change in Late Imperial China* (Cambridge, Mass.: Harvard Council of East Asia Studies, 1984). For the disappearance of the *Zisizi* text in the Southern Song, see Huang Yizhou, *Zisizi jijie* (Master Zisi, compiled with explanations), 2 vols. in seven fascicles in the series *Yilin yisi: Dier zhong* (Jiangyin, Jiangsu: Nanjing jiangshe, Southern Quintessence Academy, 1896). For nineteenth-century academies, see Barry Keenan, *Imperial China's Last Classical Academies: Social Change in the Lower Yangzi, 1864–1911* (Berkeley: Institute of East Asian Studies, University of California, 1994). Those interested in the lively Chinese-language academic revival of Confucianism, including scholarship on the indigenous origins of some Neo-Confucian ideas, should consult the careful assessment of its international dimensions in John Makeham, *The Lost Soul: "Confucianism" in Contemporary Chinese Academic Discourse* (Cambridge, Mass.: Harvard University Asia Center, 2008).

Index

Page numbers in **boldface** type refer to diagrams and illustrations.

About the Author

BARRY C. KEENAN is professor of history at Denison University and an associate in research at the Fairbank Center for Chinese Studies at Harvard University. His previous books include *The Dewey Experiment in China* and *Imperial China's Last Classical Academies*.

DIMENSIONS OF ASIAN SPIRITUALITY

Production Notes for Keenan | *Neo-Confucian Self-Cultivation*

Cover design by Julie Matsuo-Chun

Text design by Rich Hendel with display type in Tarzana Wide and text type in Minion Pro

Composition by Copperline Book Services, Inc.

Printing and binding by Sheridan Books, Inc.

Printed on 55 lb. Glatfelter Natural B18, 360 ppi